WELCOME TO ORKNE

The monuments of Orkney provide a rich
and unique insight into the past. Many of
them are accessible to visitors, and this
book explores more than 60 of the most
interesting sites. It also provides a general
introduction to the history and culture
of these remarkable islands.

The oldest monuments date back 6,000 years
to the days of the first farmers, and some of them
are very well preserved. From the earliest times,
a shortage of timber led people to build from the
workable local stone. As a result, an extraordinary
record of human activity has survived. Although
Orkney is perceived as remote today, this has
not always been the case.

This book is intended to help readers to get
the most from a visit to Orkney and experience
its amazing history for themselves.

CONTENTS

Above: The Italian Chapel, built from rudimentary materials
by prisoners of war on the tiny island of Lamb Holm.

Opposite: The interior of House 7 at the Neolithic
village of Skara Brae.

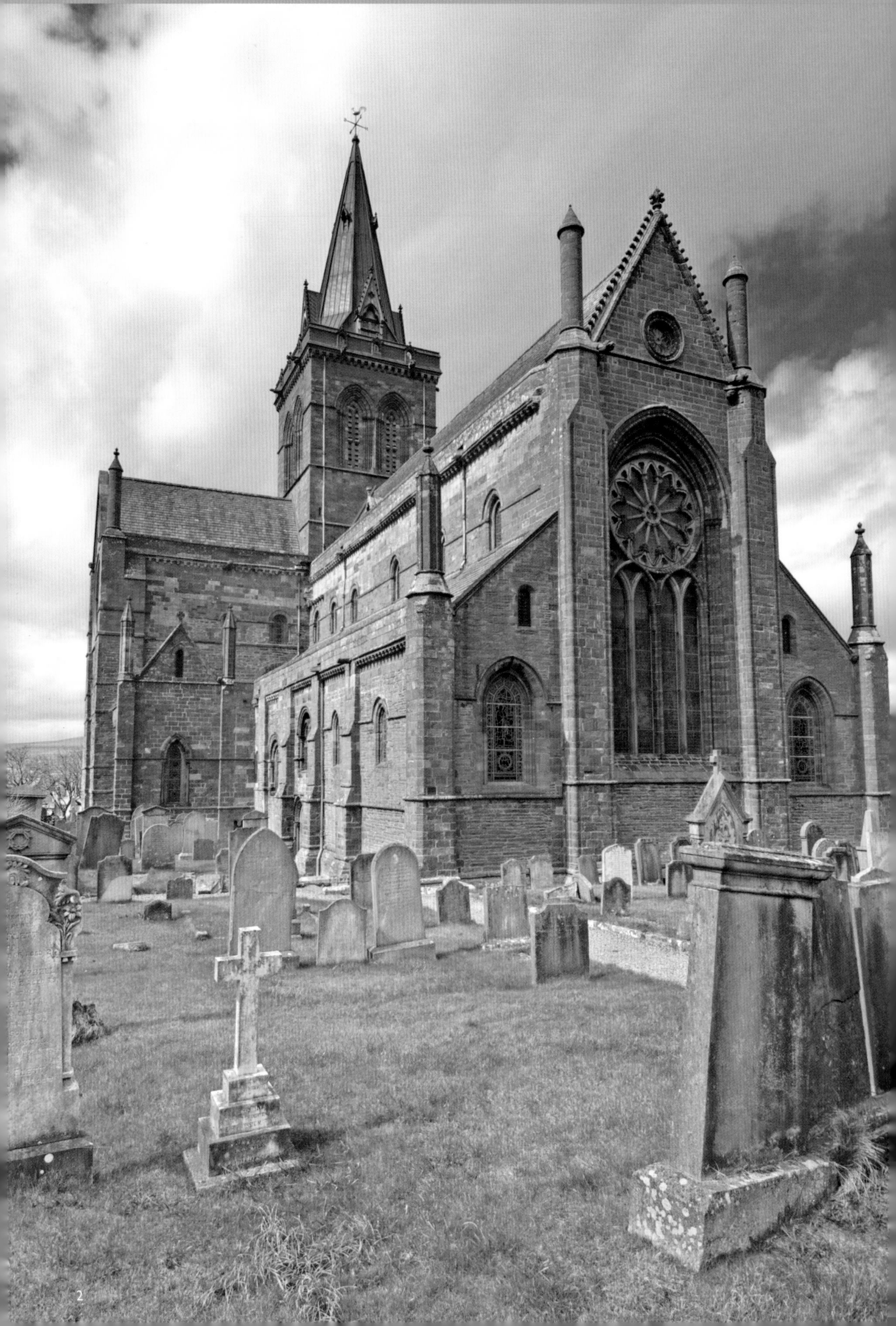

INTRODUCTION

The archipelago of Orkney, lying just four miles from mainland Scotland, is today considered remote: green and fertile, yes, but also a place of relaxation and peace. Yet in the past, when we did not live by the car and proximity to a major city was not so important, those who dwelt in Orkney were at the heart of a political and economic network that stretched across Europe. The people of Orkney have seen their fair share of action.

Orkney has been inhabited for some 9,000 years, since the arrival of Mesolithic hunter-gatherer groups at the end of the last Ice Age. The story of the people who lived here, their changing lives and communities down the millennia, is told through the remains they left behind. Compared to other parts of Scotland, those remains are plentiful; they provide an unparalleled archaeological resource and one which we can still visit in order to experience something of life in the past.

The archaeological sites of Orkney offer an unusually complete record. Elsewhere in Scotland, poor preservation means that the traces of our ancestors are rarely complete: we may have tombs but not houses; or ceremonial sites and not much else. In Orkney, through a combination of exceptional conditions and the common use of stone as a building material, the traces of all major strands of life have survived.

Visiting the monuments of ancient Orkney provides an intimate glimpse of the past. This guide is intended to help you make the most of this rare opportunity.

ABOUT THE AUTHOR
Caroline Wickham-Jones lives and works in Orkney. In 1977 she participated as a student in the National Museum of Scotland excavations at Skara Brae and since then she has worked on various sites including Links of Noltland and Long Howe. Her current research comprises a study of the changing landscape of Orkney, in particular past changes in sea level and the impact of rising sea levels on the people of the islands. She also teaches archaeology for the Flexible Degree programme at the University of Aberdeen.

Opposite: The magnificent St Magnus Cathedral, which still dominates Kirkwall nearly a thousand years after it was built.

Right: The well-defended Iron Age broch at Midhowe on the island of Rousay.

THE HISTORY OF ORKNEY

The archaeological record of Orkney comprises remains from the earliest farmers, around 4000 BC, until recent times.

Orkney was first inhabited shortly after the end of the last Ice Age by bands of nomadic hunter-gatherers, but they left little trace of their passing. In contrast, the Neolithic communities who farmed here left prominent sites like Skara Brae, Maeshowe and the Ring of Brodgar to provide an unprecedented view of life and death. Recent research suggests that Neolithic Orkney was prosperous and important, with wide-reaching connections.

Around 500 BC, the Iron Age inhabitants of Orkney built tall stone towers, brochs, as a symbol of their wealth and power. By the 9th century AD, the Picts had left a rich heritage of artwork in precious metal and stone. Christianity first came to Orkney around this time, though it was only fully embraced during the Norse period that followed.

The Norse earldom placed Orkney at the heart of political and economic affairs. By the 14th century Scottish power had taken over, and in the 16th century the Stewart earls brought new influences from Renaissance Europe. Orkney remained well connected to the wider world through the centuries that followed as many folk sought employment with companies such as the Hudson's Bay Company.

In the 20th century Orkney rose again to strategic prominence as the base for the home fleet during two World Wars.

The physical traces of the inhabitants of Orkney have much to tell us about history. Through these sites it is possible to witness many of the events that have taken place over the centuries.

Left: Inside Maeshowe chambered cairn, one of the extraordinary monuments included in the Heart of Neolithic Orkney World Heritage Site.

SETTING THE SCENE (7000-4000 BC)

More than 60 islands make up the archipelago of Orkney, of which 20 are inhabited today, though most bear traces of settlement in the past. The natural resources of Orkney are plentiful and have helped to foster a thriving community through the ages.

The Orkney islands lie in the Gulf Stream, the warmer waters of which not only brought abundant marine resources but also helped to maintain a more benign environment on land despite the high latitude – 59° North. Today the waters between the islands are treacherous, known for their strong currents and high energy. However, 9,000 years ago, when people first arrived here, the sea level was lower. Instead of an archipelago they found a single large island. Throughout the subsequent millennia, gradually rising sea levels have shaped the familiar geography of Orkney; the sea level reached its present height around 4,000 years ago.

In recent millennia, the islands have offered relatively easy access to the sea. Natural harbours and wide sandy beaches mean that a maritime culture has always been important. Nevertheless, navigation requires skill and can be dangerous. Stories of shipwreck abound and it should not be forgotten that the sea can divide as well as unite.

The relatively uniform sandstone geology of Orkney provided a natural building stone for early settlers. Other resources included fertile soils, abundant fresh water, a range of local mammals such as boar and red deer, and, initially, vegetation. Research indicates that woodland was commonplace at the time of the earliest inhabitants of Orkney. The early landscape included open grassland as well as trees; there was hazel, birch and willow, and heath lands on the higher hills and moors.

Above: Mesolithic hunter-gatherers harvesting shellfish from the bay near their settlement.

Orkney only took on its windswept, treeless aspect with the arrival of the Neolithic farmers 6,000 years ago. They cleared land for fields and grazing and inadvertently opened clearings to the impact of the wind. It is very difficult to regenerate woodland in Orkney once tree cover lessens. Some animals, such as foxes, are not present today, and may never have been found here, but the farmers brought their own stock. Domestic cattle, sheep and pigs flourished.

Prior to the farmers, Orkney was inhabited by groups of Mesolithic hunter-gatherers, communities which led a mobile lifestyle and harvested what they needed to survive from the land. It is likely that the first inhabitants of Orkney were displaced peoples, the descendants of those who, at the height of the last Ice Age, had inhabited Doggerland (a landmass on the site of what is now the North Sea). As conditions in Doggerland deteriorated, it became too wet to support the herds and traditional way of life of those who hunted them. So both animals and people scattered and moved away.

In time some arrived in Orkney, using skin or timber craft to cross the narrow waters of the Pentland Firth. They brought their old ways and tools with them, and it is interesting that recent excavations on Mesolithic sites at Links House in Stronsay and Long Howe in Tankerness have demonstrated clear similarities between the stone tools used in Orkney and those used by some of the earliest settlers in Scandinavia. Both groups may have a shared ancestry in Doggerland and the northern European Plain.

The Mesolithic population of Orkney is likely to have been small, perhaps only a few families, and we do not know whether they spent the whole year here. It is quite possible that they also travelled around the northern parts of mainland Scotland. Communities were fluid: at times a family group might live together; at other times they separated to exploit different environmental niches in different places. Occasionally, larger groups gathered, to exchange resources, gossip and partners.

The Mesolithic lifestyle was well adapted to mobility. Shelters were made of local materials such as hides and timber, easy to pack up and move on. Tools and goods were portable, and boats are likely to have played an important role. Much of the material culture was made from organic items such as wood, skins, grasses, bone and shell, so that little has survived. In Orkney the archaeological invisibility of the Mesolithic has been compounded by the rise in sea levels and the submergence of the coastal lands where they tended to settle and roam.

The Mesolithic settlers of Orkney did not build permanent monuments; they had a close relationship with the natural world within which they lived. Orkney had plenty to offer, though there is little trace of their passing. In most cases, an assemblage of stone tools, collected from the fields during ploughing, provides the only hint of a way of life that lasted for several millennia.

Right: Mesolithic flint tools found at Links House on the island of Stronsay.

NEOLITHIC SETTLERS (4000–2000 BC)

The earliest Neolithic farmers used timber to erect small permanent dwellings. Timber homesteads have been excavated at Ha'Breck on Wyre, and Wideford on the Mainland. In time, as timber grew scarce, building techniques were adapted to use stone. The local Orkney sandstone fractures naturally into slabs that are ideal for the construction of walling, slabbed floors, and even furniture. Stone buildings from the Early Neolithic have been excavated at Knap of Howar on Papa Westray, Green on Eday, and Stonehall on Mainland.

Later on in the Neolithic, villages developed. There are several Neolithic village sites across Orkney, including Pool on Sanday, Rinyo on Rousay, Links of Noltland on Westray and, of course, Skara Brae and Barnhouse on Mainland. Individual villages may have been home to as many as 80–100 people and there has been some debate as to whether village communities were the norm across Neolithic Britain. There is little evidence for village settlements elsewhere, but few places have such good preservation as Orkney. In most areas timber remains have long since disappeared. The recent discovery of a settlement of timber dwellings at Durrington Walls in the south of England suggests that larger communities may not be as rare as once supposed.

The houses of Neolithic Orkney are striking in their uniformity. Wherever they lived, it appears that the Neolithic farmers had a clear idea of what a home should be. The earlier houses are long, ovoid buildings, divided internally into two or three sections, with a central hearth and furnishings such as beds and cupboards. Later houses are more squat in shape, with a central hearth and stone-built beds. A dresser lay at the far end of the room, and other furnishings included watertight pits and storage areas. Small cells led off the central area, some of which were used as internal latrines.

The arrival of new settlers 6,000 years ago heralded a dramatic change for Orkney. We don't know how many people were involved, but in their boats they brought animals: domestic cattle and sheep, together with seed corn and a completely new suite of tools and goods. These people were farmers and they quickly settled among the fertile hills and sandy bays of Orkney.

With the arrival of farming, the face of Orkney changed. The woodland was gradually cleared and herds and crops thrived. Permanent homesteads appeared, together with fields, boundaries and trackways. In time great stone monuments were erected as markers across the landscape.

Above: Knap of Howar on the island of Papa Westray, probably the oldest surviving stone house in western Europe.

The uniformity of house design suggests a conservative, essentially egalitarian society that conformed to strict ideals. Nevertheless, there are indications that the picture was not so simple and it is important not to forget the ways in which people express themselves through decoration and detail. At Skara Brae the houses were designed to be locked from the inside, suggesting a need for personal space and privacy, while the construction and use of large stone monuments and ceremonial sites suggests the existence of some form of burgeoning social or political hierarchy.

The everyday goods of the farmers were quite different from those of the Mesolithic hunters. They included new objects and styles; fashion had changed. New tools, for different tasks, were made of stone, bone and antler, as well as wood. New materials included the use of clay to make pottery, which was often highly decorated. The earliest pots have round bases and are known today as Unstan Ware after a prominent Early Neolithic site. Later Neolithic pottery was flat-based and often bucket-shaped; it was highly decorated, and today we call it Grooved Ware.

In addition to the utilitarian needs of daily life, jewellery has been found in large quantity, often made of fine bone and including beads and polished pins with ornate heads. There are suggestions of an aesthetic side to life in the use of colour. Small pots containing pigment made of haematite and ochre were found at Skara Brae, and at Ness of Brodgar and Links of Noltland pigment was applied to parts of the walling.

The settlement sites are usually associated with midden deposits: household rubbish which was carefully managed and used in building and farming work. Today the midden is a rich source of information; analysis of animal bones sheds light on dietary habits, organic materials help us to understand the environment, information on certain plants and fungi used for medicinal purposes has been preserved.

Right: A fragment of Neolithic Grooved Ware pottery found at Skara Brae. The ornate pattern closely resembles contemporary designs found at Newgrange in Ireland.

MESOLITHIC MYSTERY

The arrival of the first Neolithic farmers brings one of the greatest mysteries. What happened to the hunters who had lived here for so many years before? Did they take on the new ways and just abandon their old lifestyle? Such wholesale change seems unlikely. The islands provided a finite resource, and one which was dwindling as sea levels rose. This was a time of great stress for the Mesolithic population as new peoples with very different ways took over and their traditional homelands disappeared.

NEOLITHIC BURIALS (4000-2000 BC)

As the new farmers became established in Orkney they began to build great monuments which served as markers in the landscape.

Massive tombs, with a central stone chamber reached by a short passage and covered with layers of clay and turf, were used to inter the bones of the ancestors and create a sense of place for each community. The early Neolithic tombs were

divided internally by upright stone slabs, perhaps mimicking the division of space inside a house. They vary greatly in size, from the majestic remains of Midhowe on Rousay, to the small mound at Unstan on Mainland. Some incorporated intricate patterning in their masonry: these sites were intended to impress.

Later tombs comprise a series of smaller cells leading off a central chamber. It has been suggested that the differences in style of the tombs reflect the more general differences in domestic architecture of the time and that the tombs should be regarded as 'houses for the dead'.

We can never know the precise meaning behind these sites, but they were clearly used as much by the living as by the deceased. They could be entered repeatedly, and, in some cases, it was possible to seal the entrance from the inside. The interior space could accommodate several living people, and the repository of ancestral bones is likely to have been only part of their function. These sites were a focus for community activity, though access may have been restricted to a privileged few, while most people congregated outside.

Above: An artist's impression of a Neolithic interment ritual.

Left: The interior of Midhowe Chambered Cairn on Rousay.

Burial rites seem to have involved activity outside the tombs, as bodies were defleshed before being placed in the tomb. In some cases this involved excarnation on platforms where birds such as eagles or ravens could remove the soft tissues. The transformation from cadaver to skeleton may have been considered highly symbolic, representing preservation of the essential spirit of the ancestors, who would then become objects of reverence for the future.

Analysis suggests that not everyone was buried in a tomb, begging two questions: where were other people laid to rest? And on what grounds was the selection made? Detailed examination of the bones from the tombs of Isbister and Quanterness suggests that many of those interred had suffered from debilitating diseases such as scurvy, though this may not have been an average sector of society.

DID YOU KNOW ...

The prevalence of scurvy in the bones from the tomb at Isbister seems surprising. Nevertheless, isotope analysis of Neolithic skeletons across Britain suggests that at this time there was a dramatic change in diet as people switched from eating marine food such as fish and seal meat, to a predominantly terrestrial diet based on cattle and sheep. Add to this the reduction of wild plant foods in favour of home-grown grain such as barley and the result is a considerable loss of vitamin C from the diet. Scurvy may simply be the result of the Neolithic farmers not eating their greens!

GORDON CHILDE AND ORKNEY

V. Gordon Childe is perhaps the archaeologist best associated with Skara Brae and Neolithic Orkney. Originally from Australia, Childe was already a prominent archaeologist in the UK when he was appointed to oversee restoration work at Skara Brae in 1928. For Childe the work was frustrating: priority had to be given to the needs of the structural work rather than the unravelling of the archaeology. But his records remain a key source of information about the site, and his findings proved to be important in a much wider field of archaeology than Scotland alone.

In the early 20th century, archaeologists relied strongly on artefact types and the assumed pace of human development in dating a site. Childe opposed the views of his fellow contemporaries and considered Skara Brae to be much older than previously thought. What he found here was to play an important role in his understanding of the development of human societies generally.

Childe was interested in examining the human past across Europe, and he brought Skara Brae to a wider stage. Through his work, the sites of Neolithic Orkney came to play a crucial role in the development of theories of world prehistory that still underpin much of our learning today.

Above: Gordon Childe at Skara Brae in the 1920s.

NEOLITHIC CEREMONIAL SITES (4000–2000 BC)

As the farming communities became established, so new types of site appeared. In addition to the great stone tombs, people were building ceremonial sites, of which the best known in Orkney are also the earliest, and most important.

Circular ditches, defined by an external earthen bank and enclosing wide platforms, were dug along the narrow spit of land that stretched between the marshy open waters of the area now known as Brodgar and Stenness. These sites are known as henges and they represent a considerable investment of communal time and effort, probably the coming together of Neolithic communities from right across Orkney.

The best known of the henge sites are the Ring of Brodgar and the Stones of Stenness, but it is possible that the circular feature surrounding the tomb of Maeshowe also started life as a henge, and there is another henge to the north at the Ring of Bookan. Together these sites make up the ceremonial heartland of Neolithic Orkney. It is striking that no other henge sites are known in Orkney, suggesting that this area was particularly important for farming communities from right across the isles.

Above: The Ring of Brodgar in the Heart of Neolithic Orkney.

With time, the henges at Brodgar and Stenness were embellished by the addition of standing stones. Today these form great circles that mimic the rounded form of the henges, but it is possible that the circle was less important than the actual act of bringing and raising the stones. The stone circles are impressive monuments today, but we see them only in their ultimate form; they underwent many years of activity before they reached this stage and their final, 'finished' appearance may be misleading.

The precise function of henge sites remains unknown, but they seem to have served as centres, probably used for many different activities, just as we use our communal spaces (churches, theatres, leisure centres) for a variety of different occasions. It is possible that at certain times access to the interior was restricted; the use of fire and smoke inside the closely spaced stones would have been quite magical to those watching from outside, especially if combined with music, colour and dance. The ditch and bank helped to demarcate the heart of the site, while at the same time the bank might aid viewing. At other times activities might have been quieter and involve fewer members of the community.

The limitations to our understanding of sites like these have been highlighted by the discovery of a new site in close proximity to the others. The site at Ness of Brodgar was clearly an integral part of the ceremonial complex, but it lay invisible until work by the Orkney Research Centre for Archaeology (ORCA) started to reveal its complexities in 2002. Ness of Brodgar represents a previously unknown type of site; it comprises a number of monumental stone buildings apparently enclosed by broad stone walls. The site is striking not just for the size and grandeur of its conception, but also for the way in which it underwent repeated re-modelling. Activity at the Ness of Brodgar seems to have taken place over a thousand years, from 3200 BC, and represents a considerable input of design and organisation. It is perhaps shocking to realise that the stone circles may only represent the visible part of sites that were originally much larger and more complex.

The remains of Neolithic Orkney are outstanding and for the visitor they evoke a strong sense of the sophistication of life in the past.

WORLD HERITAGE ORKNEY

In 1999 Skara Brae, Maeshowe, Ring of Brodgar and the Stones of Stenness were collectively designated as a World Heritage Site, also incorporating the Watchstone and the Barnhouse Stone. World Heritage status is a tremendous accolade, afforded to very few sites worldwide. There are five World Heritage Sites in Scotland, and 22 others throughout the UK.

The World Heritage Convention seeks to safeguard the well-being of exceptional sites, cultural and natural, worldwide. Potential sites are nominated by a government and the designation is awarded by a committee appointed by UNESCO. While a World Heritage designation does not, of itself, bring additional funds, it is an acknowledgement of the importance of a site and of the need to protect it. In Orkney, World Heritage designation has sparked a detailed programme of research as we seek to find out more about these sites and the wider society of which they were part.

Right: Historic Scotland's conservation team laser-scanning the Stones of Stenness, part of the World Heritage Site.

BRONZE AGE, IRON AGE AND PICTISH ORKNEY (2000 BC-AD 900)

By 2000 BC Skara Brae had long been abandoned. The introduction of a new material – metal in the form of copper, then bronze – leads us to name this period the Bronze Age, though in reality metal objects impacted little on local farmers.

Copper and bronze goods were initially scarce in Orkney, but there were other changes afoot. Village settlements seem to have been abandoned in favour of scattered farmsteads. There were new pottery types and new styles of stone tools. Craft skills developed and values in society shifted from the communal towards the individual.

There also seems to have been a change in belief and ceremony. Many ceremonial sites were remodelled and there was a shift away from the heartland at Brodgar. Further afield, new settings were erected, including large monoliths such as the Seatter Stone in Eday. Many of the communal chambered tombs were closed, while individual burials became common. Most comprised small circular settings known as barrows, but occasionally large mounds were raised, such as those by the Ring of Brodgar. At Knowes of Trotty, natural mounds were enhanced to provide a dramatic setting for burials, at least one of which included fine grave goods: a series of gold discs with intricate decoration and some amber beads. The burial at Knowes of Trotty is a clear indication of increasing social stratification. This was a significant individual. Wider links with the area around Stonehenge are also implied by the artefacts found in the tomb.

Excavations in Westray have unearthed Bronze Age houses similar to those of the late Neolithic, but other structures are different. Scattered around Orkney are burnt mounds, small stone structures with mounds of burnt stone, usually incorporating fresh water. Some were domestic dwellings; others were specialised and have been interpreted as sweat lodges or saunas. Some may have been feasting places.

By the 1st millennium BC, metal objects were more commonplace and included pieces made of iron. This facilitated the rising importance of individuals and increasing social stratification. In Iron Age Orkney, villages once again became the norm, often clustered around a prominent circular tower, known today as a broch. Brochs were built of local stone and represent a remarkable architectural achievement; some still survive to a considerable height.

Broch villages made a clear statement about the wealth and resources of a community. They were well placed to control routeways, and could also act as a defensive base. The Iron Age was a time of conspicuous wealth and this is also reflected in smaller objects. Fine metal jewellery has been found as well as weaponry and there is evidence for local metalworking.

Increasing uncertainty is reflected in the rise of defended settlements such as brochs, crannogs or island dwellings, and promontory forts. Underground chambers known as earth houses, or souterrains, date from this time, and are found across Orkney. Earth houses were usually associated with dwellings such as roundhouses and may have been used primarily for storage. The variety of Iron Age structural remains mirrors an increasing population with more complex needs.

Left: Knowes of Trotty, whose natural contours were enhanced during the Bronze Age for use as a burial site.

Communities focused on farming, but there was a strong social hierarchy: local aristocracies were able to accumulate considerable wealth. Fine metalwork has been recovered, including both weaponry and ornaments, and illustration shows elaborate styles of dress. Evidence suggests local centres of power including Birsay and Mine Howe. For the first time Orkney identified with a wider nation: the Pictish domain extended as far south as Fife and comprised many strongholds, each offering allegiance to local kings.

In the 8th century, Christianity first came to Orkney. The new religion seems to have taken hold quickly; there are several chapels with early dedications, and isolated hermitage sites such as the Castle of Burrian in Westray may date to this time.

Until recently there was little evidence for burial and ceremony in Iron Age Orkney, but the excavations at Berstness and Mine Howe have changed this. At Berstness the remains of over 100 individuals, including many newly born babies, were laid to rest around a small ceremonial structure. At Mine Howe there were few skeletons, but the emphasis lay on ritual.

Iron Age Orkney was conscious of a wider world. While the Romans never dominated the islands, there is evidence that people were aware of events elsewhere. Fragments of a Roman amphora were discovered at the Broch of Gurness, and a fine intaglio of carnelian, carved with an eagle, was excavated at the Howe.

By the 1st century AD, documentary accounts are added to the record. The name Orkney is first recorded about this time, and by the 6th century Orkney was inhabited by people with an established historical presence: the Picts.

Pictish villages and farmsteads have been recorded, consisting of cellular stone-built houses divided into individual rooms.

The Picts are known for their striking artwork. Several Pictish symbol stones have been found in Orkney. Perhaps the best known is the one from Birsay depicting three men, led by a finely dressed warrior, together with animal and geometric motifs. A new discovery from Sanday depicts a Christian cross as well as a sea creature. Similar designs occur on the metalwork of the time.

Top left: The Pictish carving of three warriors found at the Brough of Birsay. It may have been broken deliberately.

Above: A Pictish carved cross found in 2011, embedded in the floor of a cottage in Sanday.

THE NORSE EARLS (900–1050)

The late 8th century AD brought newcomers to Orkney. The arrival of the Norse heralded considerable change and would have a lasting impact.

By AD 900 there were Norse earls of Orkney whose allegiance lay in Norway, while their influence extended south to the Scottish mainland and west to the Hebrides. With its sheltered harbours and fertile fields, Orkney was well placed at the heart of a great seafaring nation.

The precise interaction between the Norse and the local Picts has been much debated and it is striking how little Pictish culture survived into the Norse period. House types changed, Pictish art was no longer produced, people abandoned Christianity for older traditions, a new language was adopted and a new administrative system and local taxes initiated. It has been suggested that the local population may have been enslaved, as an alternative to wholesale massacre. Whatever happened, little survived of Pictish ways.

Orkney had much to offer the Norse incomers and it is not, perhaps, surprising that they imposed their dominance.

Norse settlements have been found across Orkney. Dwellings were long and spacious, built of stone foundations with turf walls and roofs. Internal fittings included central hearths, flanked by benches and platforms. Animals were kept in byres, and on higher-status sites subsidiary buildings housed separate cookhouses and saunas.

Many Norsemen were farmers, living in scattered steadings, but one or two larger settlements developed. Pierowall in Westray is recorded as a thriving market centre and Kirkwall was well placed for trade: the church of St Olaf was built here about 1035. In Birsay there are remains of a large and wealthy settlement and it is recorded as a political centre before power shifted east to Kirkwall and the Cathedral of St Magnus. Smaller communities, centred on the dwellings of powerful earls, existed in places like Deerness, where the settlement occupies an isolated sea stack.

Above: An aerial view of the Brough of Deerness, at the eastern tip of the Mainland. Traces of other buildings can be seen around the surviving ruins of the Norse church.

Norse society was highly stratified and included a variety of trades and craftspeople. Farming provided a strong local basis, but those with other skills had a place. The sagas paint a vivid picture of a world where the annual round incorporated lengthy voyages as well as the regular chores of the farm. Women played an important role, often managing the farm while their menfolk were away. Wider experience and contacts were essential and therefore many of the more wealthy families sent their youth to Scandinavia and beyond in order to build connections.

Many voyages had a strong trading element, and there were specialised settlements, such as Quoygrew in Westray, where fish were processed for export to the Baltic. Imported goods included timber from Norway for houses, soapstone bowls from Shetland, and antler and whalebone, both used for a variety of domestic items such as fine bone combs.

There was also a more aggressive side to the Norse accumulation of wealth, through piracy and raids elsewhere. The Vikings were not only after precious objects. They were also active slavers, trading in markets such as Dublin or Scandinavia.

Other voyages were more political, as the Norse kings, together with the earls of Orkney, strove to maintain their power and influence. A strong Orcadian presence was recorded at the Battle of Clontarf in Ireland and in raids on Anglesea in Wales. The combination of farming and raiding was central to the Viking way of life and it is vividly portrayed in accounts of the life of Sweyn Asliefarson, who lived on Gairsay in the 12th century.

DID YOU KNOW . . .

The ancient mound of Maeshowe was entered on several occasions by the Vikings. They left an interesting legacy of graffiti on the stone walls which tells us much about their preoccupations and desires:

'Ingigerth is the most beautiful of all women'
'These runes were carved by the man most skilled in runes in the western ocean'
'To the north-west is a great treasure hidden'

THE SAGAS

The Icelandic sagas provide an important source of information about the Norse period, useful both for their account of events and for the remarkable detail of everyday life and concerns. Of particular interest with regard to Orkney is the *Orkneyinga Saga*, compiled in the late 12th century from earlier accounts and focusing on political history. Many of the locations mentioned in the saga may still be recognised; some still bear the same names. For the archaeologist it provides a rare chance to populate the excavation sites, and even name and describe some of the folk who lived here:

'This was how Svein used to live. Winter he would spend at home on Gairsay, where he entertained some eighty men at his own expense. His drinking hall was so big there was nothing in Orkney to compare with it.' (*Orkneyinga Saga*, chapter 105).

Right: A page from the Icelandic saga of Olaf Trygvesson.

THE LATER NORSE YEARS (1050-1350)

The Norse people who settled in Orkney swiftly transformed its culture. But it was not long before they had adopted the Christian religion previously embraced by the Picts they had subdued.

Christianity in the islands seems to have waned with the coming of the Norse, and the Pictish religious foundations fell out of use. But it was not long before the Norse themselves were converted.

The *Orkneyinga Saga* recounts that in 995 Olaf Trygvesson, a powerful and newly converted Norwegian, forcibly converted Earl Sigurd of Orkney aboard his ship at Osmundwall in Hoy. Sigurd was not a newcomer to Christianity. His mother and wife were both Christian, and by the mid-11th century small churches and chapels were to be found across the islands. The present parish system in Orkney has its roots in this period. Sites such as the Round Kirk at Orphir and St Magnus Cathedral survive to show how Christianity became rooted in Norse society.

Burial rituals reflected the changing times. There is a plentiful heritage of pagan burials, some of which were rich and elaborate. At Scar in Sanday three individuals (an elderly woman, an adult male and a child), were laid to rest in a small boat together with valuable grave goods. There were also pagan cemeteries, for example at Westness in Rousay. After the arrival of Christianity, simple graves clustered in cemeteries around the church sites. Grave goods were abandoned, though some burials were marked with fine carved stones.

Towards the end of the Norse period, more elaborate defended sites arose, with central keeps, typified by Cubbie Roo's Castle in Wyre. These sites are few in number, but they mark a leap in scale, also represented by the construction of the great cathedral in Kirkwall. Their grandeur is reflected in the appearance of two-storey hall-houses built by the more prosperous landowners.

Right: A bronze brooch interred as part of a Viking boat burial at Scar on Sanday.

The ability of architecture to represent wealth and power was not lost on the political elite of Orkney, and by this time the power of the Church was deeply entwined with the power of the aristocracy.

In 1231 Earl John of Orkney was killed in a pub brawl in Thurso. His death marked the end of Orkney as a Norse power, though in reality increasing Scottish influence is visible among the local aristocracy in the preceding decades. By the early 13th century the powerful Norse families had close kinsmen among the equally powerful aristocracy of the Scottish court so that on John's death the earldom passed to his near family: the earls of Angus.

Initially, the islands retained an important role in Norse affairs. There were Orkneymen at the Battle of Largs in 1263 – an indecisive yet crucial skirmish that brought an end to Norwegian claims in the west of Scotland.

In 1290 Orkney was the setting for one of the most poignant political tragedies to unfold between the kingdoms of Scotland, England and Norway, for it was here that the seven-year-old Princess Margaret of Norway died of natural causes. Margaret was granddaughter and heir to the Scottish king Alexander III, who had died not long before, and she was on her way to marry Edward, Prince of Wales, son of Edward I of England. It would have been a powerful union between the three countries, but it was not to be.

Margaret's death created a crisis in the Scottish succession which led in turn to the long Wars of Independence. It also marked the diminishing of Norwegian influence in Orkney and Scotland. In the 1320s the line of the Angus earls died out and eventually the earldom passed to the Sinclairs, another powerful Scottish family.

ST MAGNUS

Magnus Erlendson – canonised as St Magnus after his murder in the early 12th century – was a key figure in Norse Orkney. His adherence to Christian ways played a key role in ensuring the lasting power of the church in Orkney. Accounts of his life typify the aggression of the times and the rivalry between the families of the Norse earls:

'St Magnus, Earl of Orkney, was a man of extraordinary distinction, tall, with a fine, intelligent look about him. He was a man of strict virtue, successful in war, wise, eloquent, generous and magnanimous, open-handed with money, sound with advice and altogether the most popular of men. He was gentle and agreeable when talking to men of wisdom and goodwill, but severe and uncompromising towards thieves and Vikings, putting to death most of the men who plundered the farms and other parts of the earldom.'

(*Orkneyinga Saga*, chapter 45)

Above: St Magnus in stained glass at St Magnus Cathedral.

ST ROGNVALD

Born into the powerful, but troubled, dynasty of Orkney earls, Earl Rognvald grew up in Norway. He is described as a cultured man, not least through his own poetry:

'At nine skills I challenge –
A champion at chess:
Runes I rarely spoil,
I read books and write: I'm skilled at skiing
And shooting and sculling
And more! – I've mastered music and verse.'

(*Orkneyinga Saga*, chapter 58)

Rognvald was one of three Orkney earls who went to Jerusalem. He set out in 1151 and did reach the Holy Land, but the journey was not without distractions, as his own poetry shows when he reached Narbonne and met the beautiful Princess Ermingerd:

'I'll swear, clever sweetheart,
You're a slender delight
To grasp and to cuddle,
my golden-locked girl ...'

(*Orkneyinga Saga*, chapter 86)

Above: St Rognvald in stained glass at St Magnus Cathedral.

THE SCOTTISH EARLS (1350–1653)

The Sinclair earls laid the foundations for the next phase in Orkney's cultural development. It was to culminate during the ascendancy of the notorious Stewart earls.

The first Sinclair to hold power in Orkney was Earl Henry (c.1345–1400). He built a fine castle in Kirkwall, though it was destroyed in 1615. He is reputed to have been a great traveller who journeyed as far as Greenland. There is no evidence that this journey took place, though the legend reflects a growing interest in transatlantic affairs. Earl Henry was succeeded by his son, another Earl Henry, who spent less time in the islands.

In 1468 Orkney was once more thrust onto the political scene. Both Orkney and Shetland were used by Christian I of Denmark as part payment of a dowry on the marriage of his daughter Margaret to James III of Scotland. With this move, the transfer of the islands to Scotland was politically and socially complete. The Old Norse language slowly died out, and Scottish customs, such as the use of local surnames rather than Scandinavian patronyms, gradually took over.

The Sinclair family was large and powerful, and not always peaceful: in 1529 two feuding Sinclair cousins fought for control of the islands at the Battle of Summerdale in the Stenness moorlands. Concerns about local allegiance brought James V himself to Orkney in 1540. In 1565 the earldom passed to a new family, in the person of Robert Stewart, half-brother of Mary Queen of Scots.

The Stewart earldom was marked by a cultural and social atmosphere very different from the Norse domination of the preceding centuries. The Stewart earls were politically and socially ambitious. They were men of great vision, keen to demonstrate their wealth and cultural elegance through a lifestyle that drew on fashionable links with Renaissance Europe. They broadened the cultural outlook of Orkney away from its northern roots. Yet their era is remembered locally as one of particular hardship: rents and taxes were high and strictly extracted; their great building projects often relied on enforced labour.

Above: Earl Patrick Stewart in the great hall of his palace in Kirkwall, as it may have looked around 1607.

In 1569, Earl Robert started work on a fine palace in Birsay; it comprised an elegant building landscaped with gardens and was designed to make a clear statement about his wealth, sophistication and culture. In 1600 his son, Earl Patrick, commissioned another magnificent palace in Kirkwall, which is recorded to have had sumptuous interior decorations including paintings and tapestries. It was part of a scheme intended to incorporate the Bishop's Palace, which had been rebuilt and remodelled in the mid-15th century.

The reign of the Stewart earls came to a premature end. Earl Patrick could not sustain his ambitious lifestyle; he fell into debt and was eventually indicted for treason. His son, another Robert, was sent north to collect rents and debts and restore the Stewart lands, while Earl Patrick languished in prison. Robert Stewart seems to have exceeded his brief. He took control of the centre of Kirkwall – the castle, cathedral and palace – in a move that reinforced the Crown's worries about treason. After a long siege he was captured and both father and son were executed in Edinburgh in 1615.

Earl Patrick was, perhaps, just too outwardly ambitious. Others were scarcely more circumspect. Gilbert Balfour arrived in Orkney in the late 16th century; he had had a troubled life and, no doubt as a reflection of this, his castle at Noltland in Westray combined strong defences with stark aristocratic grandeur. Balfour could not resist political intrigue and was ultimately executed in Sweden.

Elsewhere in Orkney, a number of elegant houses attest to the wealth and aspirations of the time. Local lairds built fine dwellings that marked a subtle change in lifestyle, among them William Bannatyne of Gairsay, John Stewart in Eday and the Baikies of Tankerness.

But life for the average inhabitant of Orkney changed little in the 16th and 17th centuries. Survival revolved around farming, which became increasingly difficult during the 17th century. Climatic deterioration and a series of poor harvests compounded the taxes and high rents of the Stewart earls. Records suggest that many farmsteads stood empty as famine became commonplace. Nevertheless, there were good links by sea to Scotland. Imported goods from the south were valuable, as were exports. Merchants and traders were thriving in towns such as Kirkwall and Stromness.

The end of the earldom came abruptly in the early 1650s with the arrival of a Cromwellian garrison to take control of Kirkwall. St Magnus Cathedral was used as a stable, and Cromwell's troops are said to have been guilty of 'several irregularities and oppressions'. They brought new ways with them including, apparently, the first locks and keys. In general, however, the Cromwellian occupation seems to have had little impact on the life of ordinary folk. Times were hard enough as it was.

THE INDUSTRIAL AGE (1653-1900)

With the departure of the Cromwellian garrison, Orkney became more rooted into mainstream Scottish affairs. Many local landowners implemented new developments. Some brought more success than others, but in general life grew easier.

In the 18th century, the climate in Orkney improved, helping farmers rebuild. The medieval land division of runrig was replaced by a new system known as 'planking' and new crops, such as potatoes, appeared. At Cara in South Ronaldsay an ambitious cattle park was set up by Sir James Stewart in order to improve the quality of livestock.

In the 19th century David Balfour engaged a well known architect, David Bryce, to build Balfour Castle on Shapinsay, an elaborate mansion in the Scottish Baronial style. The estate also included a gasworks to provide power and a new village for the workers, complete with toilets, sited on the shore and flushed by the tide.

Other resources were exploited commercially. Kelp was collected in large quantity from the shore and burnt to produce a glassy slag that was easy to export and much in demand for its high alkali content. The kelp industry was controlled by the landowners, but provided employment for many. Up to 3,000 men, women and children were employed when the industry was at its height. Though kelp had long been harvested for use on the fields, it was first burnt commercially around 1720. The industry was introduced first to Stronsay by the laird, James Fea, but it soon spread across the isles. By 1830, nevertheless, the kelp industry was under threat from sources of potash and soda elsewhere in Europe. It experienced a brief revival later in the 19th century as a source of iodine, but by the early 20th century all that remained were the numerous kelp pits and drying walls around the coasts of Orkney.

Other work involved imported materials: in the late 18th century a local linen industry employed women at home, using imported flax from the Baltic. This was followed in the 19th century by the plaiting of straw for bonnets and other goods.

The herring industry provided employment for men, on the boats, and for women to process the fish. Several coastal villages retain relics of more prosperous days, including large herring stores and accommodation buildings. The fishing industry was important, with increasing commercialisation, but there were other types of employment available. Many ships called in to Stromness to take on fresh water before a transatlantic crossing and from the late 18th century onwards whaling became a significant employer. Both merchantmen and Royal Naval ships came into Stromness and many Orcadians entered their service.

Others travelled overseas. Throughout the 18th and 19th centuries Orkneymen were much in favour as recruits for the Hudson's Bay Company, which valued their resilience to the harsh conditions of the Arctic. Several became figures of renown – none more so than John Rae, who signed on as surgeon aboard one of the company ships and became one of the greatest Arctic explorers of his time. Rae worked closely with the Inuit populations to discover the sought-after Northwest Passage, but he is best known for unravelling the tale of the ill-fated Franklin Expedition of 1845.

Right: The toilets (with tidal flush) installed by the Balfours for their estate workers on Shapinsay.

The 18th and 19th centuries were prosperous times in Orkney. Though money from local industry went first to the lairds, the benefits permeated society. Employment was more plentiful than in many places further south and island populations remained high. Landowners used their wealth to embellish their country homes and build town houses in Kirkwall, while poorer families could occasionally afford imported luxuries such as tea.

Education was regarded as important: the records of Kirkwall Grammar School go back into the 18th century (there was a Cathedral school long before that), and the library, founded by William Baikie in 1683, was established as The Orkney Library in 1815, though it did not become a free library until 1890 following a donation by Andrew Carnegie.

The need to transport goods such as kelp and linen meant that wheeled carts were commonplace and roads and trackways were well maintained. A steamship service to the south was started in 1833, and the first regular tourists began to appear.

DID YOU KNOW . . .

In 1824 Captain William Richan of Westray and his wife moved into a new town house in Kirkwall. Shortly afterwards his wife is said to have won a wager as to who could consume the most expensive breakfast by placing a £50 note between slices of bread and eating it.

Top right: Fishing boats in Kirkwall harbour in the 1860s.

Right: A portrait of the Orkney-born Arctic explorer John Rae, together with his gold pocket watch.

A NEW CENTURY (1900–1939)

Orkney's strategic importance had been identified in earlier centuries, but its role in the world wars of the 20th century brought new focus. War brought tragedies and privations, but there were also to be lasting benefits.

When the First World War broke out, Orkney was thrust on to the world scene. Scapa Flow, sheltered between the islands south of Mainland, became the home of the British Grand Fleet in 1914. The military authorities were conscious of the vulnerability of Scapa Flow with its many entrances, and ageing coastal steamers were sunk as blockships to close access from the east. This proved an adequate defence, for now.

The fleet comprised around 35 ships, and with them came infrastructure: gun batteries, signal stations, accommodation and administrative buildings. Small islands such as Flotta saw considerable development at this time. The Orkney garrison comprised around 100,000 people, many billeted on board the ships.

Towards the end of the war the action moved into the air. The first warplanes arrived and small air stations were built. In 1918 the first strikes took place from an aircraft carrier when seven Sopwith Pups took off from the decks of HMS *Furious*.

Above: Albert Street, Kirkwall, around 1900, showing the famous 'Big Tree', a sycamore more than 150 years old.

At the end of the war, 74 ships of the German High Seas Fleet were interned in Scapa Flow, while the Allies decided their fate. Four thousand crew members arrived to maintain the ships. Their time was dominated by boredom and uncertainty, which ended on 21 June 1919, when the German admiralty issued coded instructions to scuttle the fleet, preventing its use by the Allies.

Above: A ship's telegraph recovered from one of the scuttled German ships in Scapa Flow.

Top right: Soldiers at Ness Battery, near Stromness, in 1915.

Most of the ships were salvaged and their metal is now much in demand for its purity. The salvage work brought its own personnel and prosperity, but within a few decades Britain was once more plunged into war and Orkney again became strategically important.

WARTIME SHIPWRECKS

The scuttling of the German fleet was by no means the only tragedy to strike Scapa Flow. In 1916 the HMS *Hampshire* set sail from Lyness for Murmansk in Russia. On board was Field Marshall Earl Kitchener, Supreme Commander of the British Forces. At the last minute she altered course to sail up the west coast and shortly after leaving the security of Scapa Flow she struck a mine off Marwick Head and sank with the loss of all but 12 of the crew. Kitchener was lost.

In 1917 over 800 crew members died when HMS *Vanguard* exploded at her moorings off Flotta. The cause was thought to be an internal fire near to the cordite compartments.

In 1918 HMS *Opal* and HMS *Narborough* left Scapa Flow to hunt German warships, but weather conditions deteriorated to such an extent that when neither ship returned to base it was two days before they were discovered. Both had run aground to the east of South Ronaldsay; there was one survivor.

Disaster was to strike again at the beginning of the Second World War.

Left: Lord Kitchener disembarking at Scapa Flow, hours before he was killed aboard the HMS *Hampshire*.

THE SECOND WORLD WAR AND AFTER (1939–)

By the time war broke out again, in September 1939, Orkney must have seemed well equipped for a 20th-century conflict. But it was not long before the defences were found to be tragically inadequate.

The naval base at Lyness on Scapa Flow, established in 1919, included facilities for refuelling and servicing the fleet, as well as accommodation and recreation areas for the 12,000 personnel stationed there. Elsewhere in the islands there were army camps, four airfields and a tight network of coastal defences, including batteries at Hoxa Head and Ness Battery.

But only six weeks into the war, Orkney bore witness to tragedy. On 14 October 1939, the German submarine U-47 slipped into Scapa Flow and sank the HMS *Royal Oak* while she lay at anchor, with the loss of 800 sailors. This disaster prompted the urgent deployment of improved technology and management to improve the security of the British fleet. Work soon began on the construction of barriers to seal the eastern entrances to the Flow.

The building of the Churchill Barriers was a monumental task that took years to complete. Much of the workforce was made up of Italian prisoners of war, captured in North Africa. They lived in two camps on the small islands of Lamb Holm and Burray.

Despite their labour on the barriers, the Italians found time to work on a number of social buildings within the camps. Prominent were two small chapels, of which one survives on Lamb Holm. Originally set at the heart of the camp on Lamb Holm, the chapel today sits in evocative isolation. It is constructed from a pair of Nissen huts whose unremarkable outward appearance belies the intricacies of the interior. Led by a painter named Domenico Chiocchetti, the prisoners worked to give the impression of a finely carved and decorated church.

The chapel was not finished until shortly after the war ended. It has since been adopted by the Orkney community. It is still consecrated as a place of worship and is a popular venue for weddings and concerts. Chiocchetti hoped to create a lasting monument to peace and his wishes have, surely, been fulfilled.

After the war, many buildings were removed or pressed into alternative uses. Many Orkney farms include old Nissen huts or pillboxes. Of the airfields, Grimsetter now lies under Kirkwall Airport; Hatston is a thriving industrial estate; at Twatt many of the buildings survive in local farmland and much of Skeabrae is in disrepair.

Along the coast many of the anti-aircraft batteries survive and where they are stable they make interesting coastal walks. At Ness Battery in Stromness the accommodation blocks, mess halls and underground magazines all survive alongside the command tower and gun emplacements. Within the mess, a detailed mural illustrates the yearnings of those stationed here. In sharp contrast to the religious paintings produced by the Italian prisoners, the troops at Ness Battery painted powerful scenes of English countryside.

Left: Airmen at Hatston airfield near Kirkwall in the 1940s.

The wars brought outsiders to Orkney in large numbers, and had wider repercussions for those who lived here. Roads and transport connections were improved; there was a market for local foods and jobs were created to provide for the garrison. For those who lived in the South Isles, the building of the barriers established permanent access to Kirkwall; they were no longer dependent on ferries.

Today the wartime impact on Orkney continues, including the economic benefits of tourism as visitors arrive to view the remains on land or dive on the surviving wrecks of the German Fleet. Recreational diving is now big business in Orkney.

This postwar prosperity is evident elsewhere too. Local foods, jewellery, knitwear and other crafts, music and artwork all thrive. In the 1970s the Flotta Oil Terminal ensured that the islands' central role in economic affairs would not diminish and in recent decades this has been upheld. A flourishing industry in renewable energy has developed, including the generation of both wind and wave power. But those who live in Orkney are well aware of the power of their history as well as the benefits for the future.

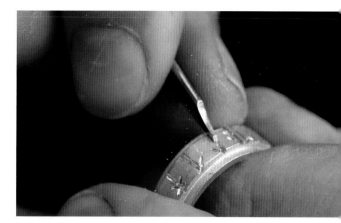

Above: Making rings at Aurora Jewellery near Kirkwall, part of Orkney's thriving jewellery industry.

ARCHAEOLOGY: THE NEW PROFESSION

Orkney in the 21st century boasts a high density of archaeologists. In the 19th century the discovery of key sites like Skara Brae helped to shape contemporary understanding of human history, and later the work of Gordon Childe put Orkney archaeology onto the world stage. Since then Orkney has welcomed many eminent academics keen to unravel the secrets of its past.

In 1999 Orkney College, part of the University of the Highlands and Islands, opened an Archaeology Department and now it is possible to train locally. Many students stay to pursue their careers and, facilitated by modern communications and easy transport, others arrive to settle locally. The monuments of Orkney are remarkable not only for their quality, but also for their quantity, and their study and management affords interest for those who wish to make Orkney their home.

Right: The ongoing archaeological dig at Ness of Brodgar (see page 44).

VISITING ORKNEY'S MONUMENTS

This section provides individual information on key sites. The aim is to help the reader plan a visit to Orkney, and get the most from the sites to be explored.

The sites are organised by period and function: prehistoric settlement sites are followed by ceremonial sites and then tombs. Pictish and Norse sites comprise both religious monuments and domestic remains. The vagaries of archaeological preservation mean that from this time on most remains relate to high-status activities and families.

The importance of the Church is reflected in the number of small kirk sites across the isles. The palaces of the Stewart earls reflect their short-lived Renaissance ambitions, while the increasing influence of Scottish power is seen among the houses and castles of the 16th and 17th centuries. In the 19th century, the changing fortunes of local agriculture emerge, while many of the 20th-century remains are marked by the footprint of war.

Each site is identified by island, and for Mainland sites the mileage by road is given from Kirkwall or Stromness (whichever is closer). A directory on pages 87–9 gives more detailed location information.

Left: The Broch of Gurness overlooking Eynhallow sound at the north of the Mainland.

PREHISTORIC: DOMESTIC

SKARA BRAE

Mainland, 7 miles N of Stromness

Skara Brae provides an unusually intimate view of life in Neolithic Orkney. The remains of several houses survive, but it is the furnishings and material goods that make this site remarkable.

The site was first discovered in 1850 when a great storm blew away the sand that had lain over it, and from the start it was recognised as something special.

The village comprised a group of dwellings set back from the sea and surrounded by farmland. The houses were built from a double skin of stone, with midden (decomposed refuse) packed into the cavity to provide stability and insulation. The doorways open to a central passageway that was roofed over with stone slabs. This passage served to allow movement about the settlement without going outside.

Each house comprised a single room, about 6m by 6m, divided into separate zones. At the centre lay the hearth. On the wall opposite the door stood a stone dresser. To either side there were stone beds and other furnishings. Beside the dresser there were small, watertight troughs that may have been used to keep food or bait fresh.

The walls survive to roof height, but there is no precise evidence for roofing materials. Recent research suggests that the houses had steeply sloping roofs covered with tough waterproof vegetation such as eelgrass. The roof may have been supported using timbers from driftwood (more abundant than today), or perhaps whalebone. Within the walls of each house lay one or more small cells. These were probably used for storage, but some had drains, suggesting that they were latrines.

Above: The Neolithic village of Skara Brae at Skaill Bay on the west coast of the Mainland.

Skara Brae has been investigated on many occasions and under varying conditions, so it is hard to be certain about everything that was found there. The artefacts resemble those from other Neolithic sites across Scotland, but thanks to Skara Brae's unusually good preservation conditions, elements absent elsewhere are often represented here.

In addition to stone tools of flint and chert, the inhabitants made and used clay pottery. Their pots were flat-bottomed and varied in size from tiny pinch pots to great bucket-like containers. Many were highly decorated – a style of pottery known as Grooved Ware. The people who lived here also used tools of bone and antler.

The occupants were probably families, perhaps combining three or more generations. Dwelling in a single room seems a difficult concept today, but there are ways to make it work. At Skara Brae the interior space may well have been used in a highly regulated fashion, with different people allowed access to different parts of the room. It is also possible that different activities were kept to different spaces. Most tasks were probably undertaken outside when the weather permitted.

There are no windows, and with the passageway outside the door the interiors must have been dark. Light would come from the fire, and animal fats may have been burned in lamps, though curiously none have been positively identified.

One building stands apart. Structure 8 is also connected by the passageway, but sits slightly away from the houses. The door opens from a small porch to a main room where there is a central hearth, but the dresser and beds are absent. There are various recesses and niches, suggesting that this may have been a workshop of some kind, an idea supported by the complex flue opposite the entrance. Gordon Childe, who excavated Skara Brae in the 1920s, recorded worked chert in large quantity here, as well as debris from pottery manufacture.

Farmland surrounded the village and provided grazing for livestock: cattle, sheep and pigs. Crops were grown, though cultivation was difficult in the later stages of occupation, probably due to increased salination of the soil. The residents fished, collected shellfish and trapped sea birds. Red deer were hunted, and wild plants gathered.

Life was not just about survival. There was time for personal adornment and many items of jewellery have been found, made of animal bone and animal tooth. In addition there are indications of the use of colour: small pots of ochre pigment and haematite rubbing stones. Many examples of art have been found around the settlement. Most comprise finely incised lines on the stonework, some are pecked. The motifs are geometric and also occur on pottery and bone work. While their original meaning is lost, it is clear that these designs were recognisable and meaningful to the villagers.

Skara Brae was inhabited for some 600 years between 3100 BC and 2500 BC. During this time coastal erosion bought the sea gradually closer and salt spray and wind began to affect the farmlands. Life grew more difficult. The precise reasons why the site was finally abandoned remain unclear, but it is likely to have been more mundane than the original story of inundation by sand during a terrible coastal storm. Terrible coastal storms are well known in Orkney, but recent archaeology has not unearthed any evidence that people had to flee overnight.

Right: One of the carved stone objects found at Skara Brae. We do not know how they were used.

BARNHOUSE VILLAGE

Mainland, 5 miles NE of Stromness

Barnhouse is a Neolithic village, occupied between 3200 BC and about 2900 BC. These dates coincide with the early centuries of occupation at Skara Brae, but there are important differences.

The houses here survive only as the footings of stone walls. They were of similar shape and design to those at Skara Brae but there is no evidence for linking passageways. Each house contains a central hearth, stone beds and dressers, though there are no cells of the kind found at Skara Brae. Similar objects were found at Barnhouse, though less organic material has survived. There were tools of flaked stone and Grooved Ware pots, some of which were beautifully decorated.

Barnhouse also contains two structures that are very different from the others. House 2 is larger than the rest and seems to have two rooms. There are two hearths, to either side of the entrance. Each half contains three wall recesses, resembling beds. Post holes suggest other features, but there are no dressers.

Structure 8 is the biggest in the settlement and seems to have been built right at the end of the activity here. It is a completely different construction,

Above: House 2 at Barnhouse Village.

comprising a circular clay platform, on which stood a large rectangular building. A circular drystone wall enclosed the complex. The entrance does not line up with that of the central building: people would have been forced to move around the platform to reach the heart of the complex.

There are other hints that this was a special place. On reaching the entrance to the central building people found their way blocked once more, this time by a large hearth that may have provided some sort of purification. Inside lay another hearth, at the centre of the complex, and beyond that a stone dresser.

Structure 8 combines elements from the Neolithic dwellings, such as the dresser, with more ritualised elements such as the complex access arrangements. It also has links to more obviously specialised monuments such as the Stones of Stenness. There are close similarities in design and layout between the two sites and it has been suggested that hearth slabs from Structure 8 may have been moved to the Stones of Stenness.

Barnhouse may have been more than just an ordinary village; certainly, those who lived here would have been very familiar with the great stone monuments that were in use nearby.

KNAP OF HOWAR

Papa Westray

Knap of Howar represents the earliest evidence of Neolithic settlement in Orkney. A single farmstead, it was occupied sometime between 3500 and 3000 BC.

Two buildings survive, linked by a cross passage. The larger seems to have been the dwelling and is divided by stone slabs into two rooms, each with various furnishings including benches. There was a central stone hearth in the inner room. The smaller building was divided into three and served as a byre and workshop. There was a hearth in the central room and the furnishing included recesses and shelves.

Both structures had an entrance at one end, in addition to the cross passage that joined them. The walls stand to their original height, though there is no trace of the roof. Stout driftwood beams or whalebone ribs must have supported a sloping roof of thatch, seaweed or turf.

Like Skara Brae, Knap of Howar was very well preserved, under a capping of shell sand. The finds included tools of stone and bone, together with pottery of an earlier form, round-bottomed Unstan Ware. There were also abundant deposits of midden which provided information on diet.

The inhabitants cultivated barley and reared cattle, sheep and pigs. In addition they fished and harvested local shellfish and seabirds. They probably hunted red deer.

Tantalisingly, the early midden levels at Knap of Howar indicate that an even earlier settlement must have existed nearby, though no trace of this has been found.

Today, Knap of Howar stands at the edge of the sea, in danger from the full force of winter storms. This was not the case when it was inhabited, however. The evidence suggests that Papa Westray and Westray may have been joined across the shallow waters that lie between them.

Knap of Howar has been linked with the early Neolithic tomb 1.5 miles away on the tiny island of Holm of Papa Westray to the east (see page 52). It may well have provided the resting place for the bones of the ancestors of those who lived in the steading. Excavation has shown that the tomb was in use during the life of the settlement so it must have been familiar to them.

Above: The residential space at Knap of Howar, with the byre/workshop beyond.

LINKS OF NOLTLAND

Westray

The remains at Links of Noltland date from two periods of occupation: Neolithic and Bronze Age. Unusually, the site includes evidence from both periods in close proximity.

The earliest evidence dates to about 3000 BC. After this the site seems to have been abandoned, though it was later re-occupied. There are at least six Neolithic houses, similar in size and shape to those at Skara Brae, but freestanding, like those at Barnhouse. Most survive only as stone footings, with traces of internal hearths and furnishings, but at least one had been dug down into the sand so its walling survived to a greater height. Many of the houses have been subject to alteration and rebuilding.

Structure 9 hid an interesting secret: within the cavity of the walls, 30 cattle skulls encircled the building. They would have been invisible, but the slaughter of this number of cattle would have been a noteworthy act for a community who relied on their stock for survival. It would only have been undertaken for significant reasons.

Another building, Structure 8, yielded a stone figurine about 4cm high. Dubbed the 'Orkney Venus', she is intricately incised with detail to represent arms, clothing, and maybe even hair. When she was found in 2009, no similar examples of human figurines were known from Neolithic Scotland, but since then other figurines have been recognised elsewhere and a second found at Noltland.

The well preserved finds represent a remarkable record of everyday life: fine bone pins and beads complemented the stone tools and elaborately decorated pottery. Wide spreads of midden have also provided detail about the economic life, diet and environment of the early farmers.

The Bronze Age settlement comprises at least eight oval stone buildings, probably the remains of two or more farm steadings. Each steading comprised three buildings – a dwelling and a workshop set close together, and a building that may have been a byre. The dwellings are paved, with central hearths, internal settings, furnishings and recesses. The entrance lay at one end, opposite the workshop. The workshops were more specialised. One had a carefully laid clay floor, while another contained a large, stone-lined tank.

The dunes at Links of Noltland are rich in archaeology. Elsewhere human bone has been discovered, the remains of Iron Age burials.

Top: The 'Orkney Venus' figurine found at the site.

Left: Archaeologist Sean Rice with the ox skulls found at Noltland in 2009.

LIDDLE BURNT MOUND

South Ronaldsay

A Bronze Age structure of uncertain purpose, Liddle is one of a number of burnt mounds identified on the islands.

Liddle was first recorded as a mound of burnt stones and earth about 2m high. Excavation revealed a stone-built structure, dated to the Bronze Age. The building was oval in plan, and measured 6.5m by 4m internally with an entrance at one end. Inside, it was subdivided into compartments. At its heart lay a large stone tank, and there was a hearth set into an alcove in the wall. A gully ran away from the tank to the outside of the building. There were low stone walls that may have been topped with turf and the whole is likely to have been roofed with thatch of reeds, heather or grasses.

The finds from Liddle comprised sherds from large, bucket-shaped pots, as well as various sandstone hammers and pounders. Analysis suggested that the main source of fuel was peat.

Above: The burnt mound at Liddle, possibly used for cooking in the Bronze Age.

Archaeologists are divided as to the precise interpretation of the site at Liddle. It is clear that heating and possibly cooking were important, and some see burnt mounds as domestic in nature. Others prefer a more specialised, perhaps even ceremonial, explanation. John Hedges, who excavated Liddle, drew attention to the farming landscape within which it lies, and interpreted it as the remains of the cooking place of a small Bronze Age farmstead.

MEUR BURNT MOUND

Sanday

Although much of its burnt material has been lost, the mound at Meur has certain features in common with the better-preserved site at Liddle.

Meur lies on the foreshore at the north end of Sanday and was uncovered by winter gales in 2005. An emergency excavation revealed the structural remains of a burnt mound, from which much of the characteristic burnt material had long since disappeared.

The remains at Meur comprise a large stone trough at the centre of a structure defined by low stone walls. The building appears to have been subdivided into compartments, as at Liddle, and there was a drainage system and a cistern associated with the trough.

Finds from Meur were sparse – not surprising, given the location of the site on the foreshore. There were a few broken sherds of pottery and chipped flints. A quantity of fish bones had been preserved within the fills in the trough and elsewhere. Bones from cattle, sheep and various birds were also recovered.

Above: The team of archaeologists during work at the Meur Burnt Mound site.

In contrast to Liddle, the walls at Meur comprised simple slabs, set vertically. They would not have supported a roof of any sort. This site has therefore been interpreted as an outdoor cooking place dating to the late Bronze Age (about 1000 BC).

TOFTS NESS

Sanday

Tofts Ness is more than just a single site; it comprises the well-preserved remains of an archaeological landscape. It was occupied by a small community of subsistence farmers. A number of mounds can be seen, together with smaller cairns and earthen banks.

The Bronze Age inhabitants of Tofts Ness may have visited Meur, which was in use at the same time. However, the remains at Tofts Ness cover a longer period, from the Neolithic until well into the Iron Age.

Investigation of one mound here revealed the remains of a small farm, a circular stone dwelling with a steeply sloping thatched roof. Inside, the building was divided into several rooms. The main steading was remodelled and altered on several occasions, but occupation seems to have been continuous.

The remains of various field banks attest to the skill and daily routines of the prehistoric farmers. They cleared stones to create land for cultivation, piling them into small clearance cairns. A sophisticated system of manuring, using midden mixed with ash, maintained the fertility of the sandy soils, enabling the cultivation of barley. Livestock included cattle, sheep and pigs.

This northern landscape was not an easy place to survive, and the occupants made full use of the wild resources to hand. Farming produce was supplemented with fish from shore and lochan, shellfish, seabirds and wild plants.

Tofts Ness provides an interesting contrast with other prehistoric sites in Orkney. Its marginality may have been social as well as economic. The finds from the site suggest that the inhabitants were of lower social standing than their counterparts on other excavated sites.

Tofts Ness is not laid out for the visitor, but the landscape as a whole is striking. In addition to the settlement mounds, the remains of a burnt mound were excavated. There were small clearance cairns and field walls, and also burial mounds. One of the small cairns contains two Bronze Age cists and one of the larger mounds may have been a Neolithic chambered cairn. This was a living, working landscape. It reminds us how, for the everyday farming family, death and the memory of death were a part of life.

Above: An artist's impression of the subsistence farming community at Tofts Ness.

GRAIN EARTH HOUSE

Mainland, 1 mile NW of Kirkwall

Above: The interior of Grain Earth House.

An underground space, probably used
for storage, the earth house at Grain is
a particularly well-preserved example.

This earth house, or souterrain, lies about 2m
below the ground surface and comprises a curving
passageway that leads to a rounded chamber in
which four upright stones support the flagstone roof.
The walls of the passage and chamber are built of
drystone and a short flight of steps leads down from

the present-day ground surface at the far end
(the upper part of this stair is modern, rebuilt
when the site was taken into State care).

Grain was discovered in 1827, and investigated in
1857 by local antiquarians Farrer and Petrie, who
discovered it to be empty, though there were traces
of domestic settlement around the entrance on the
surface of the ground. Today only one earth house
survives here, but excavation in 1982 uncovered a
second, smaller earth house nearby, together with
the remains of Iron Age buildings suggesting there
had once been a small Iron Age settlement.

It is likely that the site was in use in the first
millennium BC. The lack of finds makes it hard
to be precise about the function of earth houses.
They are generally assumed to have been built for
storage, though recent research has highlighted the
importance to Iron Age society of underground
chambers for many different purposes, one of
which may have been ritual.

RENNIBISTER EARTH HOUSE

Mainland, 5 miles NW of Kirkwall

This earth house was discovered by accident
in 1926 when the roof of the chamber collapsed
under the weight of a threshing machine in
the farmyard above. Investigation revealed the
remains of at least 18 people in the chamber,
including 12 children.

Rennibister Earth House is entered via a modern
hatch and metal ladder that lead directly to the
chamber. The original passageway may still be seen,
but is too low for modern access. The oval chamber
has drystone walls and a corbelled roof, supported
on four upright stones. Set into the chamber walls
there are five recesses and various shelves.

Few earth houses have yielded skeletal material in
such quantity, but recent research has shown that it
is far from unusual. Iron Age society was complex
and the archaeological information from the
period is correspondingly intricate. It is unlikely
that earth houses served a simple function and of
course their role may have changed with time.
The deposits at Rennibister seem to relate to a
period towards the end of the life of the site.

The earth house is likely to have been built in the
first millennium BC and served a local settlement,
perhaps the precursor of the present farm.

Above: Two of the uprights supporting the
corbelled roof at Rennibister Earth House.

BROCH OF GURNESS

Mainland, 15 miles NW of Kirkwall

The remains at Gurness date to the first millennium BC. They housed a substantial Iron Age community of some status.

The focus is the central stone tower or broch, which would originally have reached about 10m in height. Its interior is divided into compartments by fine upright slabs. The tower comprises two skins of drystone walling, between which lie stone-floored galleries, accessed by steps. A stone ledge at first-floor level suggests that there was once a timber floor here. The whole would have been covered by a thatched roof, with the stairs continuing to a wall walk at the wall-head.

There are two hearths and an internal cistern, with steep stone stairs running down to it. It is not possible to access this today, but it bears a striking resemblance to the stair and cistern at Mine Howe. It may relate to the Iron Age cult of the underground.

The site is protected by three rock-cut ditches with stone ramparts. Between the inner ditch and the tower lie the remains of numerous small stone houses. These were built after the tower, but the settlement was clearly planned as a whole. Several houses open from a main 'street' that runs from the outer entrance to the broch.

Brochs were once considered to be defensive structures, and the outerworks at Gurness would support that, as would the substantial bar-holes that secured the entrance. Gurness is well placed to control traffic along the Eynhallow Sound, but it is more than a simple defensive tower. The broch itself was an indication of the wealth and status of the local chief. Evidence for this is provided by finds of imported amphora from the south, perhaps bringing sweet wine or olives.

Settlement at Gurness continued into the 5th century AD, into Pictish times. At this time the main broch tower had fallen from use and the stone was plundered to build a series of smaller dwellings on top of the earlier remains. Even later, in the 9th century AD, a stone-lined grave was created for a Norse woman, laid to rest with a fine pair of bronze brooches and an iron sickle and knife.

Above: The imposing entranceway at the Broch of Gurness.

Above: The entrance to Midhowe Broch, accessible only via a sturdy outer forework.

MIDHOWE BROCH

Rousay

This broch occupies a commanding situation on Eynhallow Sound, across the water from Gurness. At Midhowe, too, the central tower is surrounded by a settlement of small stone houses.

Midhowe Broch lies in a naturally defensive position on a steep coastal promontory, with two ditches and a stone rampart cutting off access from inland. The remains of the tower stand over 4m high and there are internal galleries. Its interior is divided into two rooms, each with a hearth, though some of the internal fittings are later. Each room has a cistern, one of which is still fed by a spring.

Unusually for Orkney, the ground floor gallery runs right around the interior of the walls. This feature weakened the structure, and at some stage it was blocked and an external buttress built to strengthen the tower.

The outer buildings at Midhowe have suffered from coastal erosion, and only a fragment of the settlement survives. It must have been a high-status place, however. Excavations in the 1930s found evidence for the manufacture of metal artefacts including bronze jewellery. Other finds suggested that craftwork included weaving. There were also several objects of Roman origin, indicating contact with communities further south.

Eleven brochs line the shores of Eynhallow Sound – this must have been an important route for Iron Age Orkney. These were farming communities with connections far afield. In addition to their own produce, they were able to draw on a wider world and the market for luxury goods was slowly developing.

BURROUGHSTON BROCH

Shapinsay

Although still partly immersed in the grass mound that concealed it for centuries, this broch has retained clear evidence of robust defences.

Until 1862 Burroughston was nothing more than a grassy mound. Excavation took place in that year, but the broch retains the impression of being semi-subterranean because much of the mound was left in place.

The broch tower survives to first-floor height. The walls were over 3m thick, and the entrance passage attests to the need for security. There is a guard chamber and the door could be locked: the checks and bar-holes are well preserved. Inside the broch there are traces of internal fittings and divisions made of stone, as well as the entrance to a deep well. A second cell opens at ground-floor level opposite the door and the stone ledge to support the first floor is visible around the walls.

The broch was encircled by a ditch, to either side of which there were stone ramparts. Traces were found of a settlement between the broch and its defences, but these are now grassed over. Evidence of later activity on site was also recorded and no doubt helped obscure the original remains, as did the depredations of the sea.

Above: An aerial view of Burroughston Broch, with circular features just visible in the grass around the site.

PREHISTORIC: CEREMONIAL

This page: Three of the Stones of Stenness, each with its steeply angled top.

THE STONES OF STENNESS

Mainland, 5 miles NE of Stromness (Part of the Heart of Neolithic Orkney World Heritage Site)

The Stones of Stenness probably represent some of the earliest activity on the Brodgar peninsula, at the epicentre of Neolithic Orkney.

Western Circle of the Stones of Stenness

Radiocarbon dating indicates that work on the monument had started by 3100 BC. At this time the settlement at Barnhouse was well established and the ceremonial site at the Ness of Brodgar was under construction.

This was originally the site of a henge: a level, circular platform surrounded by a ditch with an external bank. Even without the standing stones it was an impressive monument, with a ditch that was over 2m deep and 7m wide. Inside, there were probably various features that could be adapted depending on the ceremonies taking place. At the heart of the site lies a great stone hearth. This has been linked to a similar hearth in the ceremonial hall at Barnhouse. It is a reminder of the sparse nature of archaeological remains: a massive fire within the henge would have brought colour, movement and warmth.

At some stage deep foundations were dug for 12 massive standing stones, the tallest of which is over 6m high. It seems likely that these were erected over a considerable period of time, perhaps generations. Excavation in the 1970s suggested that at least one socket was never filled. While the plan of the site was fixed in advance, the actual work may have taken decades.

The stones have sharply angled tops. Standing near the centre of the circle it is possible to see how the two largest stones angle towards one another and mirror the hills of Hoy on the horizon. We can never be certain of the intentions of the builders, but this may be a good example of a Neolithic community locating and designing a monument to relate to the wider landscape.

Near the hearth stand the remains of a dolmen-like structure: two upright slabs that used to support the horizontal stone beside them. This monument was toppled in the 1970s, at which time there was great debate as to its authenticity. Excavation was unable to resolve whether or not the 'dolmen' had formed part of the original design.

To the north-west, on the shores of the Loch of Stenness, stands the Watchstone. There were once at least two stones here. In the 1930s work on the road uncovered the stump of a second upright by the side of the loch.

A third stone stood between the Watchstone and the site: the Odin Stone stood in the field to the north of the henge. This monolith, pierced by a sizeable hole, was destroyed in the early 19th century when the local farmer decided to clear the stones. His actions proved unpopular and were stopped, but not before he had caused considerable damage.

Top right: An 18th-century engraving of the Odin Stone (right, pierced with a hole), which was destroyed in 1814.

Right: The Watchstone, a single standing stone guarding the causeway at Stenness.

THE RING OF BRODGAR

Mainland, 6 miles NE of Stromness (Part of the Heart of Neolithic Orkney World Heritage Site)

This is a classic henge site, with a ditch surrounding the platform, and an outer bank. Twenty-seven of 60 possible standing stones survive, set around the circumference.

The henge is 104m in diameter, and recent excavation across the ditch by Orkney College showed just how impressive it was when first dug. It is cut into bedrock, over 3m deep and 10m wide. There are two opposed entrances, with causeways across the ditch.

The original nature of the ring remains obscure. The level platform inside the ditch has not been investigated by excavation, and geophysics has yielded little detail. The ditch seems to have been dug in sections and it has been suggested that it was constructed by workforces from different parts of Orkney. The stones may have been erected later, perhaps over a considerable period of time. These monuments had a long lifespan and the form in which we see them represents only their final stage.

Many of the stones at Brodgar have been re-erected in recent centuries, so it is hard to interpret the precise relation of the site to the surrounding hills, but all of the surviving uprights have a characteristically angled top, and the ring is likely to have been carefully sited in relation to the horizon.

Above: The Ring of Brodgar seen from above.

Right: The runic inscription found on one of the stones.

To the south-east stands a single monolith, the Comet Stone. This may have been part of a larger setting and it reminds us that the ring is itself part of a greater complex of sites along the peninsula. There were many burials focused around the site during the Neolithic and into the Bronze Age. The four largest: Plumcake Knowe, Fresh Knowe, South Knowe and Salt Knowe were dug into long ago; recent geophysics work on Salt Knowe suggests that it does not contain any internal structure and may have held a different significance when first raised.

Today, the carving of graffiti is forbidden by law, but the stones at the Ring of Brodgar have been engraved in the past. In addition to a rich record of personal names, local and from further afield, one of the smaller stumps to the north bears Norse runes (the name Bjorn) and a small cross. To the east a taller slab holds a small engraving of an anvil.

This page: A striking view of individual stones around the henge.

NESS OF BRODGAR

Mainland, 6 miles NE of Stromness

Although only recently discovered and partly excavated, this ceremonial complex is among the most exciting discoveries of recent years, and may yet prove to be the most important monument in the whole Neolithic landscape.

Until 2002, the existence of the Ness of Brodgar was completely unknown. The first hints occurred when geophysics revealed a series of strong anomalies indicative of prehistoric activity. This was confirmed the following year when a stone slab was pulled to the field surface by a plough. The scale of the site was not revealed until 2004. Further excavation has since revealed a complex of stone buildings, in use at least between 3200 BC and 2200 BC.

To the north, it was separated from the Ring of Brodgar by a wide wall. The structures lying within the complex include several oval buildings, each divided into paired angular segments. Alongside these, and partially overlying one of them, stood a massive ceremonial hall, Structure 10.

The hall is over 25m long by 20m wide. A rectangular outer wall, up to 5m wide in places, enclosed a rounded interior structure with an internal hearth, bays and fittings. To the south stood another massive stone wall, apparently bounding the land towards the Stones of Stenness.

The stonework at Ness of Brodgar is finely worked. Considerable skill clearly went into design and construction, and there are indications of frequent alteration and rebuilding. The complex was certainly of the highest status – and smaller details have confirmed this. An unusually high number of incised stone slabs were found and there have also been examples of pecked art. Excitingly, traces of colour, probably from haematite and ochre, have survived on some of the stones. Elsewhere, stones of different colours were combined for effect.

Within Structure 8, deposits of finely split slabs suggested the use of stone roofing. The smaller finds all point to the status of the site; they include sherds from finely decorated pots, small stone axes, maceheads, objects made from whalebone and deposits of cattle bone, perhaps from ceremony or feasting.

The excavations have only touched the tip of the iceberg; geophysical surveys have indicated a considerable depth and complexity of remains here. This, perhaps more than anywhere, was the Heart of Neolithic Orkney.

Above: A reconstruction of the complex as it may have looked in around 2700 BC.

MINE HOWE

Mainland, 5 miles SE of Kirkwall

The remains at Mine Howe provide the unprecedented opportunity to descend a flight of steep stone steps into the underground world of Iron Age Orkney.

Mine Howe was not opened to the public until 1999, but was first uncovered in 1946. The local farmer was investigating a deep hole into which one of his cattle had disappeared. The site's dominant feature is a central hillock. This would have been all the more impressive when in use, because of the deep, stone-lined ditch which surrounded it. A central shaft is preserved within the mound. Inside the shaft, a stone stairway leads to an underground chamber, 7.4m below the summit. This shaft is a complex structure, which turns back on itself at a half-landing where two short side galleries emerge.

The mound formed the central feature of the complex, but the remains are more extensive. The ditch seems to have served an important role in demarcating the heart of the site from activities that took place outside. A narrow causeway provided access to the centre. Outside the ditch, geophysical work and excavations by Orkney College have revealed a series of structures including considerable evidence of metalworking.

Much of the metalworking was associated with a large roundhouse that continued in use into the Pictish period. Several small kilns had been set into its interior and it seems to have been used for bronze working: fragments of moulds, crucibles and even an ingot of copper were found inside, together with anvil stones and whetstones. The area outside the roundhouse, in contrast, yielded abundant evidence for ironworking. Inside the ditched enclosure a small iron furnace had survived largely intact within its pit. The site may have been demarcated into separate areas for bronze working and iron working.

Mine Howe was clearly an important centre. Access to the main mound seems to have been carefully controlled, and the presence of metalworking may well have provided an almost magical touch. It was certainly a high-status activity.

The sounds, smells and sights of Mine Howe provided a considerable focus for Iron Age Orkney and the site's significance is enhanced by the discovery of three human burials here. This is an interesting find, given the paucity of human skeletal material from the Iron Age in general.

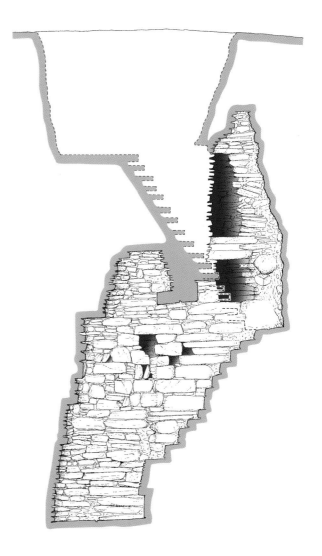

Above: A cross-section of the stairway leading to the deep underground chamber at Mine Howe.

PREHISTORIC: BURIAL

MAESHOWE

Mainland, 5 miles NE of Stromness (Part of the Heart of Neolithic Orkney World Heritage Site)

This prominent mound in the Neolithic landscape conceals an ingeniously constructed chamber aligned to the midwinter sunset.

The mound may not always have been Maeshowe's main feature. It is raised on a circular platform, demarcated by a ditch and an external bank, which may have been a henge before the tomb was built. Recent excavations have uncovered traces of stone structures that may pre-date the platform. Clearly Maeshowe was an important location of long standing. The tomb is thought to have been in use around 2700 BC, though work may have started around 3000 BC.

At its heart stands the great chamber, built of local flagstone. While the stone lent itself to this use, construction on such a grand scale was no mean feat. The first step seems to have been the erection of the four great standing stones at the corners of the chamber, which may originally have stood as freestanding uprights.

Above: The interior of the chamber at Maeshowe, with cells to left and right and the entrance passage centre.

The entrance passage is about 7m long and about a metre high; it restricts access in a way that contrasts sharply with the chamber beyond. At the entrance, a triangular stone is set into a niche in the wall; this could be drawn forward to block the passage. The passage is lined with great stone slabs running almost its full length, which would have required skilled engineering to set into place.

The central chamber is 3.8m high; originally it would have been a little higher. In Norse times, and again in recent centuries, Maeshowe was entered through the roof. A white-painted concrete cap now takes the place of the original corbelled vault. Inside, however, all remains much as intended by the original builders.

The interior wall faces are carefully built of slabs that were worked and meticulously positioned to provide a smooth, dressed surface. Small chocking stones keep the individual courses level. Apart from the entrance wall, each of the walls is pierced by a single side cell. The cell walls are built of the same dressed stone as the central chamber, but their floors and roofs are formed of massive single slabs, not unlike the side walls of the passage.

Above all is the turf-covered mound. Immediately overlying the chamber, an inner stone core provided stability and protection, but above this there are layers of clay and stones, rising to a height of 7m. This capping structure was designed to keep the chamber dry, and it succeeded, though damp has since penetrated by way of the damaged roof and 20th-century concrete capping.

Maeshowe comes alive at the midwinter solstice. For a few days every December, the setting sun shines from the horizon above the hills of Hoy, across the top of the Barnhouse Stone, down the passage and onto the wall at the rear of the main chamber, where it illuminates the entrance to the back cell. It is a theatrical reminder that the wider landscape forms an active part of the monument.

Maeshowe would have been a dominant landmark in the Neolithic landscape. It seems to have been the only tomb built on this scale, suggesting that it played a pivotal role in Neolithic Orkney. Sadly, traces of the original contents have never been found but activities probably included the veneration of the ancestors through reverence of their bones.

The design of the tomb suggests that access to the central chamber was limited to certain members of the community, though the surrounding platform may well have formed a space where others could be present. The tomb was clearly designed to be closed off and re-entered on separate occasions and it seems to have been in use for a considerable time. The proximity of Maeshowe to the other monuments along the Brodgar peninsula suggests that it formed part of the great central complex of Neolithic Orkney.

Long after Maeshowe had ceased to function as a focus for Neolithic activity it caught the attention of the Norse inhabitants of Orkney. We know that sites such as this held considerable interest for them, not least because they might contain treasure. There is a record in the *Orkneyinga Saga* that the mound was entered in the 12th century and this is confirmed by a remarkable collection of Norse runes that were carved into the walls inside.

Many of the runic messages are strikingly similar to the sort of graffiti one might find in a bus shelter today: boastful inscriptions about the prowess of the carver, or the merits of local women. They shed light on Norse society as a world where literacy was commonplace.

Curiously, five of the inscriptions mention treasure, though metal would have been unknown to the Neolithic builders of the tomb. There is, however, a hint that the writers were not just fantasising. Archaeological work has indicated that the external wall around the ditch was rebuilt in the 9th century AD and some see this as evidence that the tomb may have been re-used in early Norse times for the burial of one of their leaders. If so, perhaps the burial goods included treasure, later removed by the tomb-raiders.

Above: An exterior view of Maeshowe as a mound on the Neolithic landscape.

UNSTAN CHAMBERED CAIRN

Mainland, 2 miles NE of Stromness

The tomb at Unstan was probably in use in the Early Neolithic period, but it has features that set it apart from most tombs of that era.

The mound is entered through the original entrance passage, which leads to a long drystone chamber. The chamber is divided into stalls by thin upright slabs and the stalls at each end had horizontal stone 'shelves'. A small side cell opens from the wall opposite the entrance.

Unusually for an early tomb, the rectilinear chamber contrasts with the circular mound. The inclusion of a side cell, in addition to interior stalls, is also unusual. The communities who built the tombs were working to their own specific designs and needs.

The bones of several individuals were found within the stalls, together with sherds of at least 30 round-bottomed vessels in a style now known as Unstan Ware. There were also stone tools, including flint arrowheads. The side cell contained two bodies, buried in a crouched position, a procedure not practised in the Neolithic. It seems Unstan was in use after burial traditions had changed.

One lintel has been inscribed with Norse runes, together with more recent graffiti, reminding us of the fragility of these sites and the alterations that have taken place over the millennia. The walls survive to head height, and were capped in the 1930s by a modern concrete dome. This helps recreate the enclosed space, but the skylight and ventilation holes have created an atmosphere very different from that conceived by the original builders.

Top left: Unstan Chambered Cairn, which is still accessible via its original entrance passage.

ISBISTER CHAMBERED CAIRN

South Ronaldsay

This cairn is also known as the Tomb of the Eagles, thanks to some intriguing bird remains discovered along with the human bones.

Isbister tomb combines three side cells with interior stalls and shelved end compartments, within an oval mound. It was built in the late 4th millennium BC, and continued in use until about 2500 BC. The roof was then removed and the chamber filled with rubble.

The tomb was discovered in 1958 by local farmer Ronnie Simison. He excavated it after observing work at Liddle Burnt Mound, which also lay on his land. Inside, a wealth of well-preserved deposits included the remains of over 300 individuals, providing much information about the lifestyle and health of the Neolithic community. Grave goods included stone tools and Unstan Ware pottery.

The human bones had been separated into specific deposits. Inside the central chamber most of the bones were found on the floor; other groups of skulls lay within the two cells in the long wall.

Scattered among the human bone, and apparently included as deliberate burials, were the remains of white-tailed sea eagles. The birds may have held totemic significance, perhaps associated with the de-fleshing of bodies after death.

Isbister occupies a commanding position, high on the cliffs above the North Sea. Outside the entrance lay an amphitheatre-like space that was found on excavation to contain the remains of smashed pottery and animal bones. This suggests it was used for ceremonies, perhaps involving the wider community.

Above: An Unstan Ware bowl of the kind discovered inside Isbister Chambered Cairn.

CUWEEN HILL CHAMBERED CAIRN

Mainland, 6 miles W of Kirkwall

The tomb at Cuween Hill contained dog skulls, which may have held significance comparable to the eagle remains at Isbister.

This cairn is built into a steep hillside with impressive views over the Bay of Firth. At ground level, the chamber is cut into bedrock and side cells open from each of the four drystone walls. The entrance passage is low and narrow, but the central chamber and side cells are higher. Each cell is raised slightly above ground level, and the openings are small, but it is possible to stand upright within them.

The interior walling is finely dressed. Today it stands to a height of over 2m and is capped by a modern concrete dome, but in the past it would have been slightly higher.

Cuween Hill was excavated (not for the first time) in 1901. The remains of at least eight people were found, together with many animal bones.

The excavators found 24 dog skulls on the floor of the central chamber and this has been interpreted as a totemic deposit that may parallel the eagle bones at Isbister.

Excavations in the 1990s uncovered the remains of a small Neolithic village at Stonehall, immediately below Cuween Hill.

Above: The cairn at Cuween Hill, cut into the bedrock and found to contain 24 dog skulls.

WIDEFORD HILL CHAMBERED CAIRN

Mainland, 2 miles W of Kirkwall

Above: The entrance to the cairn at Wideford Hill.

Erosion of the mound at Wideford Hill allows the visitor to see something of the framework of stone walls supporting a Neolithic burial cairn.

This tomb also dates from the third millennium BC. It looks out over the Bay of Firth, to the west, and, like Cuween Hill, was cut into bedrock to provide a level platform for the chamber. Within the circular mound, three cells open from a central chamber, which is accessed today through the roof as the original entrance passage is long, low and narrow.

Wideford Hill has been excavated on several occasions, notably by Flinders Petrie in the 1840s. He did not find any human remains and surmised that the tomb had been deliberately infilled with rubble before being abandoned.

Today, the remaining mound does not fully cover the structure so that it is possible to see the way in which inner revetment walls of stone were used to provide stability to the tomb.

MIDHOWE STALLED CAIRN
Rousay

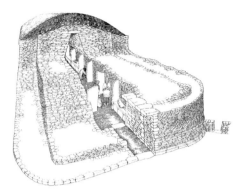

Nothing of the mound remains at Midhowe, but the great stalled cairn has been laid out under a hangar, so that it is possible to see considerable detail of its construction.

The tomb dates to around 3500 BC and was excavated in the 1930s. It comprises a long (23m) central chamber divided by upright slabs into 12 stalls on each side. Many of the stalls contain the remains of low 'shelves' or benches.

The bodies of 25 individuals were discovered on, or below, these benches, within the north-east part of the chamber. Each individual had been laid to rest facing the central space with their back to the outer wall.

The chamber was entered through a short passage to the south-east which appears to have been deliberately blocked when the tomb went out of use. At this time, or possibly later, two further burials were made, in opposite corners of Stall 4.

On the outer wall it is possible to see the way in which slabs were set at an angle to give a fine herringbone effect to the exterior. The Neolithic community of Rousay were accomplished stonemasons.

Above: A cutaway illustration exposes the structure of Midhowe Stalled Cairn as it may have looked when in use.

BLACKHAMMER STALLED CAIRN
Rousay

The tomb at Blackhammer has decorative masonry, in the form of triangular motifs on the exterior, a feature characteristic of Rousay.

Inside, the chamber is 13m long, divided into seven stalls. The original entrance opens to the south, in one of the long sides of the chamber, but today the tomb is accessed through the roof.

Blackhammer dates to the third millennium and was carefully blocked when it went out of use. It was excavated in the 1930s, at which time the remains of two individuals were found, one in the stall at the western end and one in the blocked entrance. These burials seem to represent the last activity inside the tomb.

At some time during its life the tomb seems to have been altered. Four of the upright dividing slabs were removed to make way for rough walling at the heart of the central chamber, dividing it into two.

Left: The interior of Blackhammer Stalled Cairn.

TAVERSÖE TUICK CHAMBERED CAIRN
Rousay

This burial cairn comprises two separate, chambers built one on top of the other. It was built into a steep hillside sometime in the third millennium BC.

The lower of Taversöe Tuick's two chambers is cut into the hillside and was entered from downhill. It is divided by uprights into four cell-like shelved compartments. The upper chamber was entered from uphill and comprised two compartments, one larger than the other. The hatch that connects the upper chamber to the lower one was not present in prehistory.

Both upper and lower chambers contained human bone, including skeletal material and cremated bone. In addition, three stone cists had been built inside the upper chamber at a later stage. These have since been removed.

Right: The interior of Taversöe Tuick Chambered Cairn, showing the entrances to the upper and lower chambers.

The lower chamber has a considerably longer entrance passage than the upper chamber. At its outer end a 'mini' chamber has been constructed, divided by four tiny uprights. During excavation this was found to contain three Neolithic pots, but there was no human bone. It is clearly associated with the main tomb. Experts have speculated that it may have linked to a drain-like feature that runs along the passage in order to 'communicate' with the ancestors in the chamber above.

KNOWE OF YARSO
Rousay

Knowe of Yarso occupies a prominent position at the edge of a flat geological shelf, from which the land drops sharply down towards the sea. It was built in the early third millennium BC and incorporates the Rousay trademark decorative outer stonework.

The entrance passage opens to the south-east at one end of the long central chamber, which is divided by uprights into four compartments. Unlike some of the other tombs, the passage does not appear to have been blocked.

Knowe of Yarso was excavated in the 1930s and contained the remains of at least 29 individuals, including 15 skulls that lined the floor with their faces turned towards the interior. Many grave goods were found, including pottery sherds, stone tools, arrowheads and animal bones. Among the latter were bones from at least 36 red deer. These may have been a totemic deposit.

Right: The interior of Knowe of Yarso.

QUOYNESS CHAMBERED CAIRN
Sanday

Above: The 4m-high interior walls of Quoyness Chambered Cairn.

This tomb's external appearance gives little idea of its original grandeur, but it does demonstrate the skill of the architects.

The cairn would once have been covered with a grassy mound rising well above the stone platform surrounding it. The entrance passage is only partly roofed, so we can see the two retaining walls that gave it stability. The chamber stands to its original height of 4m, though it is no longer roofed. Six side cells open from the central chamber.

Much skeletal material was recovered during excavations: some lay inside the cells, but a circular stone-built cist in the corner of the central chamber contained the remains of at least 10 adults, perhaps a later deposit. Many cairns may be seen on the peninsula around Quoyness and some are Bronze Age. This was a significant place for the prehistoric inhabitants of Sanday.

VINQUOY CHAMBERED CAIRN
Eday

This is a Maeshowe-style tomb with four side cells leading from the central chamber. Today a clear plastic roof covers the chamber; originally it must have stood at least 3m high.

Vinquoy Cairn was cut into a sloping hillside and commands an impressive position. It is built of Eday sandstone, which has a slightly rougher fracture than other Orkney sandstone. This is reflected inside, where the walling is less regular than elsewhere, though no less accomplished. The tomb was excavated in 1857 and there is little record of finds from the site.

Left: The Maeshowe-style interior of Vinquoy Chambered Cairn.

HOLM OF PAPA WESTRAY
Papa Westray

Above: The eyebrow-shaped carvings at Holm of Papa Westray.

There are two tombs on this tiny islet, distinguished as Holm of Papa Westray South, and Holm of Papa Westray North.

The one to the north is earlier, a stalled cairn that was in use from around 3500 to 2900 BC. The chamber is divided into four compartments and contained the remains of at least eight individuals. There was also evidence for continued activity after burial had ceased.

The southern tomb is of the Maeshowe style, entered today through a hatch in the modern concrete roof. The entrance passage is long and low and the central chamber has 12 side cells. Several slabs in the interior have pecked Neolithic art, including a lintel bearing curved 'eyebrow' designs. These are similar to the eyebrow features on the Links of Noltland figurine (see page 34). This tomb was excavated in the mid-19th century and there is no clear record of the material found inside.

THE DWARFIE STANE

Hoy

The Dwarfie Stane is unique in the UK, but parallels from elsewhere in Europe suggest that it was carved, as a Neolithic burial monument, sometime in the third millennium BC.

The monument comprises a huge block of red sandstone, over 8m long and 2m high, into which a short passage has been carved, with two interior chambers opening to either side. The exterior of the slab has been left untouched, but inside it is carefully worked, and the marks of the original tooling can still be seen on the roof of the southern chamber. A large blocking stone lies by the entrance and records show that this was in place, and sealed the interior, into the 16th century.

The Dwarfie Stane has always attracted interest and at some point a hole was broken through the roof to gain access to the interior (it is now restored). It features in early guidebooks to Orkney, provided inspiration to Sir Walter Scott for part of his novel, *The Pirate*, and is well known for the graffiti, in Persian and Latin, carved by a Major William Mounsey in 1850.

Left: The Dwarfie Stane – a tomb carved from a single block of sandstone.

KNOWES OF TROTTY

Mainland, 12 miles NW of Kirkwall

Twelve prominent barrow mounds add grandeur to this high-ranking Bronze Age burial site, but recent geophysical survey and excavation by Orkney College show that it was once considerably more complex. There may originally have been up to 20 barrows, flanked by the sites of pyres, enclosures and pits.

The largest barrow lies to the northern end of the group and was constructed on top of a natural mound in order to enhance it. Excavation in the 19th century revealed a stone cist, or coffin, at the heart of the mound. It was flanked by tall upright slabs, and contained cremated human bone, together with four gold discs, amber beads and pendants. Quite apart from the wealth which this must have represented, it is interesting for the links to other parts of the UK, in particular Wessex in the south of England, where the objects may well have originated. This was clearly the burial of a very high-status member of the community.

Radiocarbon dating at the site indicates that it was in use in the early second millennium BC. The complexity of the remains suggests that Knowes of Trotty was a significant burial centre for Bronze Age Orkney.

Above: The four gold discs found at Knowes of Trotty, which suggest that the deceased had both wealth and connections in southern Britain.

PICTISH, NORSE AND MEDIEVAL

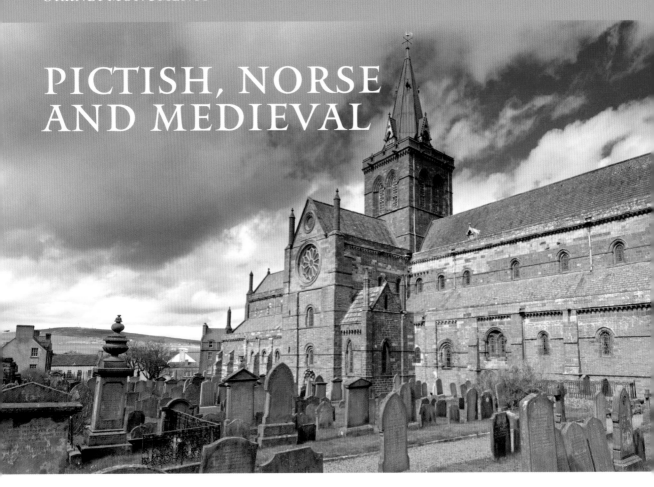

ST MAGNUS CATHEDRAL

Mainland, central Kirkwall

St Magnus Cathedral dominates Kirkwall, and is visible from far afield – both at sea and from other islands. Nine hundred years after building work started, the cathedral's siting and design bear witness to the skill and ambitions of those who built it.

The cathedral is also remarkable for the human story that lies behind it, much of which is recorded in the *Orkneyinga Saga*. Work began in 1137, inspired by Earl Rognvald's desire to honour God and celebrate his accession to the earldom of Orkney. His route to the earldom had involved removing his second cousin, Earl Paul Hakonsson. Founding the cathedral was also a pragmatic gesture on Rognvald's part. It was designed to bolster local support by furthering the popular cause of his uncle, St Magnus. (Magnus had himself been earl of Orkney until his murder by Earl Paul around 1116.) It also helped Rognvald to consolidate his influence by moving the centre of power to Kirkwall, where he was in control.

The supervisor of building work was Rognvald's Norwegian father, Kol Kalisson, Magnus' brother-in-law. He clearly intended to create a building of some magnificence, employing masons who had experience from Durham Cathedral and Dunfermline Abbey. Many masons' marks can be seen inside the cathedral, incised into the stonework at the time of construction.

A location was chosen at the rear of the existing town, near the shore (which reached further inland at the time). Work started at the eastern end and within about 15 years the choir was ready for use – though the project was halted shortly afterwards due to the deaths of Earl Rognvald and his bishop, Bishop William. In 1188 Bishop Bjarni resumed construction, on a more ambitious scale. In all, the building took three centuries to complete. The west end of the nave was not added until the late 15th or early 16th century.

Above: St Magnus Cathedral, Orkney's crowning achievement of Norse architecture.

The long period of construction is visible in small details of the design, which changed as work progressed. The pillars of the nave change in shape from east to west, and there are two styles of arch: early rounded Romanesque arches contrast with later pointed Gothic arches. In general, however, the building holds good to the original intentions of Kol Kalisson and Earl Rognvald. The combination of red and yellow sandstone, from local quarries, was used to striking effect.

In time the shore receded from the cathedral, but the original proximity of the sea was not ideal for such a big structure. In recent years the west end has been found to be unstable. Remedial work was carried out in the 1970s, during which the root cause was found to be poor workmanship, rather than actual subsidence.

The cathedral's interior bears witness to the significant role it has played in the life of the community. Tombs and sculptures line the walls. From the start the bones of St Magnus were interred here, together with those of Earl Rognvald, who died in 1158 and was himself canonised in 1192. These bones formed powerful relics and access to them was carefully controlled. At some time they were moved into cavities built within the two rectangular piers at either side of the choir.

The bones bear testimony to violence. St Magnus' skull shows a wound consistent with the description of his death in the *Orkneyinga Saga*, while St Rognvald's bones also show signs of wounds that parallel accounts of his death.

Also marked by monuments are the Orcadian explorers, John Rae, home from the Arctic (see page 23), and William Baikie, who led three expeditions to the Niger.

The fortunes of the cathedral have reflected those of the wider world. Catholics, Episcopalians and Presbyterians have all worshipped here. When Cromwell's garrison occupied Kirkwall in the 1650s the cathedral housed both soldiers and their horses. It has seen market stalls, and was threatened with destruction shortly after the failed rebellion of Robert Stewart, son of Earl Patrick. It was initially controlled by the Norwegian archbishopric of Trondheim, but supervision eventually shifted to the province of St Andrews in Scotland. St Magnus was only awarded its own parish in 1560, and curiously the building itself belongs to the people of Kirkwall, having been transferred by James III in a charter of 1468.

Maintenance of its fabric has been a major task. One problem lies in the soft nature of the sandstone used for its construction. Considerable work took place during the 19th century, including the relocation of memorial panels that had accumulated on the floor, to reveal the original bases of the pillars. A new scheme began in the early 20th century, which included further clearance of the interior. At this time the tall steeple was erected, the pulpit was installed and new flooring was laid.

Today the cathedral is a well-loved focus for community activity, both religious and secular. It provides a historic backdrop for school services, local concerts, and an annual flower festival. In 1987 a new stained-glass window was commissioned to celebrate its 850th anniversary. One of the building's most visited spots must be the memorial to the 833 crew members of HMS *Royal Oak* who died in 1939 when she was torpedoed in Scapa Bay.

Left: Lifelike carved heads adorning the cathedral's interior walls.

THE BISHOP'S PALACE

Mainland, central Kirkwall

The Bishop's Palace stands close to the cathedral, and the lower storey probably dates to Norse times. It is likely that the palace was built as a residence for Bishop William, a contemporary and friend of Earl Rognvald.

When the cathedral was built, the centre of ecclesiastical power moved from Birsay to Kirkwall. The bishop and his entourage therefore needed a new home. The 12th-century Bishop's Palace was designed to reflect the status of its occupants. It comprised a rectangular hall-house with storage and workshops on the ground floor, a main hall and dwelling quarters above. There was probably a high-pitched timber roof, similar to that of the King's Hall in Bergen, though no trace survives. Buildings like this inspired many wealthy Norse nobles to create new and more comfortable houses for themselves.

The palace was a fine building that made use of the same decorative coloured stonework as the cathedral. It provided a backdrop to the unsuccessful attempt by King Haakon of Norway to maintain control over western Scotland. Norwegian forces were driven off at the Battle of Largs in October 1263, and Haakon's fleet returned to Kirkwall, where he died two months later.

It seems Bishop William's fine palace fell into disrepair within a century. The advent of both famine and plague made the 14th century a difficult time in Orkney. The ruined palace at the heart of Kirkwall was not restored until the mid-16th century.

In 1540 James V visited Kirkwall and the palace was pressed into service as a garrison for his troops. About this time a new bishop arrived, Bishop Robert Reid (who went on to found Edinburgh University). Bishop Reid set about rebuilding the palace as an elegant residence. He added a round tower, known as the Moosie Tower, and restored and enlarged the original structure.

Bishop Reid died in 1558, and in 1568 the palace passed to Earl Robert Stewart. His son, Earl Patrick, later built a new palace for himself in this part of Kirkwall, incorporating the Bishop's Palace into it.

A niche on the outer wall of the Moosie Tower contains a statue of St Rognvald. This is a modern replica; the original is now housed in the Orkney Museum.

Above: The Bishop's Palace, with the distinctive Moosie Tower right of centre.

CUBBIE ROO'S CASTLE

Wyre

This was a fine stone castle, one of the earliest to survive in Scotland. Only the lower courses of its stonework remain, but it is an atmospheric site to visit.

The stronghold was built by Kolbein Hruga, a wealthy landowner in the mid-12th century. He chose his site well; Wyre is a low-lying island and the castle was set on a low hill surrounded by marshland. It comprised a small stone tower, of perhaps no more than three storeys, set within two rock-cut ditches. An earthen rampart was raised around the outside, and between the ditches there is a stone wall.

The main entrance to the enclosure lay to the east, across a flagstone 'bridge'. At the centre of the defences the tower walls survive to first-floor level. They are roughly 2m thick and lack any means of entrance; access to the tower required a wooden ladder to the first floor. Inside, further ladders led up and down; at ground level the tower contained a tank for water and this floor would have been used for storage.

The original castle may have been quite simple; there were later additions including external domestic buildings and wings for the tower, but these were not so robustly built and have not survived to any height.

Hruga's castle was built at a time when building work flourished in Orkney. Inspired by the construction of the cathedral and other buildings in Kirkwall, wealthy landowners raised structures on a scale that had not been seen before. At the same time, the potential for local violence, petty rivalries and aggression meant that a castle like this might be put to good use. Though it was not large, and may only have been occupied in times of trouble, the new castle on Wyre was notable. It is mentioned in the *Orkneyinga Saga* as 'a really solid stronghold', and the *Hakonar Saga* describes it as particularly hard to attack during a siege in 1231.

Above: The walls of the tower at the centre of the castle still stand to first-floor level.

THE BROUGH OF BIRSAY

Mainland, 13 miles N of Stromness

The Brough of Birsay is on a small island, separated from the Mainland by a natural tidal causeway. Settlement of this spot goes back to Pictish times, though the extensive remains visible today date to the Norse period.

The earliest activity on the site may date to the 6th century, when a small monastic establishment was founded here. Traces of the chapel and graveyard lie beneath the Norse buildings, together with oval Pictish houses dating to the 7th and 8th centuries. Above the ground, only the well survives. Fragments of a Pictish symbol stone were also found.

Birsay was a significant location in the Pictish period. Evidence for metalworking has been found, including the manufacture of fine bronze jewellery, which is only found at high-status sites. Support for this is provided by a Pictish symbol stone, which includes symbols, a mythical beast and an eagle above three finely-dressed warriors (see page 15). The first of these men is depicted with fancy curled hair and a fringed cloak. We do not know the precise purpose of the stone, but it clearly celebrates wealth and sophistication.

The stone was found in fragments outside the present kirkyard; it seems to have survived after the Pictish period but may well have been deliberately smashed at a later date. A modern cast has been set at the original site of the stone, whose fragments are held in the National Museum of Scotland in Edinburgh.

We do not know what happened to the Pictish settlement, but by the 9th century the occupants of Birsay were Norse and it was soon to rise in significance. Prior to the rise of Kirkwall in the 12th century, Birsay was the centre of power in Orkney.

The most prominent remains relate to the kirk, a small Romanesque building which dates to the 12th century and was dedicated to St Peter. Inside, the remains of a stone bench for the congregation line the walls and within the semi-circular apse stands an altar of red sandstone, reconstructed during excavation in the 1930s. Outside the kirk an enclosure wall separates the graveyard from the settlement beyond. To the north lie the remains of buildings thought to be houses.

The Norse settlement comprised a number of dwellings, some of considerable size and wealth. Not all would have been in use at the same time, but there was clearly a substantial community here. The buildings included substantial hall-houses, and evidence survives of both heating and drainage systems, together with the possible remains of saunas.

Above: The remains of a Romanesque church built at the heart of the community in the 12th century.

Right: A stone at the Brough of Birsay, incised with a Christian cross.

The *Orkneyinga Saga* records that Earl Thorfinn built a minster, known as the Christchurch, in Birsay on his return from the Holy Land in the mid-11th century. The relics of St Magnus were initially laid to rest here after his murder in 1116. The remains are of such scale and wealth that it was once suggested this may have been the location for Earl Thorfinn's hall and church. However, they are now thought more likely to have been located on the Mainland around the sheltered waters of the bay to the south.

Both the mainland bay and the brough were significant centres for Norse settlers. They had much to offer: a sheltered harbour, easy access by sea and land, fertile land, fresh water and a sheltered location for settlement. While the remains on the Mainland have disappeared under more recent settlement, those on the Brough of Birsay provide an evocative reminder of the scale of Norse settlement here.

THE BROUGH OF DEERNESS

Mainland, 12 miles east of Kirkwall

The remains at the Brough of Deerness date back to Pictish times, though the visible structures relate to the remains of the stronghold of a Norse chieftain.

The Brough of Deerness is an impressive sea stack, accessible today, as in the past, by a steep, winding path that is not for the faint-hearted. At the centre of the summit stand the stone walls of a small rectangular chapel. This was originally founded in the 10th century, and the first building was of timber. It was later rebuilt in stone and would have formed the heart of a small community for whom Christianity was important.

Around the chapel lie the remains of over 30 dwellings and outbuildings. The Brough of Deerness was long thought to be a monastic site, but excavations have yielded evidence that it was the home of a wealthy chieftain. The small graveyard outside the chapel includes burials of children. High-status artefacts were found, and the buildings include dwellings of retainers.

Recent finds of a stone gaming board and some of the antler playing pieces shed intimate light on life at the top of the stack. Dates suggest that the first Norse settled here in the early 10th century and the settlement survived well into the 12th century.

There is evidence for a rampart of stone and earth across the landward face of the stack. While outwardly defensive in nature this may also have acted as an indication of status. The site occupies a prominent position on the eastern approaches to Orkney and would have been visible from both sea and land. Norse society was showy and aggressive and the location was well chosen on both counts.

Prior to the construction of Norse homes on the stack, Deerness was home to a Pictish community. Recent excavations have uncovered evidence for Pictish dwellings: the later buildings were set into their ruins. The relationship between the Pictish and Norse settlements remains unclear.

Above: A fragment of finely carved bone comb found near the Brough of Deerness.

ORPHIR ROUND KIRK AND EARL'S BU

Mainland, 9 miles SW of Kirkwall

The round kirk at Orphir is the only surviving circular medieval church in Scotland, built around 1120. Today only the semi-circular apse stands, at the heart of the graveyard. Nearby lie the remains of a large Norse drinking hall, the Earl's Bu.

Orphir Round Kirk was reputedly built by Earl Hakon Paulsson, who had visited the round Church of the Holy Sepulchre in Jerusalem while on pilgrimage to atone for the murder of his cousin St Magnus. A small Romanesque window remains at the eastern end of the apse, together with the footings of the altar. The church's large circular nave was demolished in 1757, when stone was needed for the construction of a new parish kirk.

The Earl's Bu was a drinking hall of some status and speculation has linked it with Earl Hakon himself. The Orkneyinga Saga provides a detailed account both of the Earl's Hall, and of the activities (mainly drinking) that took place there. The remains have been investigated by excavation but there is no conclusive proof that church and hall were in use at the same time.

The excavations also revealed the remains of a horizontal water-mill. This dates back to the Norse period and would have been an important feature of the farm here. It is the earliest evidence for this sort of mill in Orkney.

Left: The distinctive curved apse of Orphir Round Kirk.

QUOYGREW

Westray

Above: An aerial view of Quoygrew clearly shows the layout of the Norse farmstead.

Quoygrew was occupied from the 10th to the 20th centuries, but visitors to the site can explore the reconstructed remains of a 12th-century Norse hall.

The site started out as a humble turf-built farm. Over time, as the occupants grew wealthier, they built in stone and added different features to their home so that it grew in complexity.

Large amounts of fish bone found in a midden on the shore nearby suggest that the Norse occupants of Quoygrew supplemented the results of farming with specialised fishing activities. The main catches were cod and saithe, popular not only for the local market but also to export as dried fish to growing urban centres further south and around the Baltic. This, no doubt, contributed to Quoygrew's increasing wealth.

Excavation yielded evidence of a medieval farmstead which overlay the Norse remains and just inland of the Norse hall lie the remains of a 19th-century farmstead. This was only abandoned in 1930, testament to changing times and changing lifestyles.

EYNHALLOW CHURCH
Eynhallow

Eynhallow is today uninhabited, but the *Orkneyinga Saga* suggests that there was a monastic settlement here in the 12th century. The well-preserved remains of a small Romanesque church have survived on the south-west shores of the island.

The existence of this church was unknown before 1851. At that time, the island was abandoned after an outbreak of fever. As the roof was taken off the dwellings to prevent re-occupation, the church was discovered, having been adapted and converted into a range of houses.

The church today stands to roof height. Though it has been much altered, the grandeur of the original design is clear. The rectangular building houses a nave and chancel, divided by a striking arch, and with a substantial porch at the west end.

The name Eynhallow means 'Holy Isle' in Old Norse, and some authorities have suggested that there may have been an even earlier Pictish monastery here, though there is no structural evidence for this.

Today it is an atmospheric site to visit, evocative of the early church and of the families who lost livelihood, loved ones and homes to the fever.

Left: Eynhallow Church, concealed for centuries within a range of domestic houses.

ST MARY'S CHAPEL
Wyre

The small Romanesque chapel on Wyre was built in the later 12th century, probably by the same Kolbein Hruga (Cubbie Roo) who built his castle close by. Alternatively, it may have been the work of his son Bishop Bjarni, who became a significant figure in the early history of St Magnus Cathedral.

The walls, partly restored in the late 19th century and since consolidated, stand almost to the wall-head. A round-arched doorway leads into the nave, which is separated from the small, square chancel by another round archway. There is no eastern window, but three small windows admit light from the south.

During the 19th-century restoration work, a grave within the chapel was found to contain the remains of a tall, well-built man, perhaps Kolbein Hruga himself. Outside lies the graveyard (today with a modern extension to the south).

The presence of the chapel and castle on Wyre, taken together with the recorded figure of Kolbein Hruga, suggests that Wyre was the location of a wealthy Norse estate. This idea is supported by the nearby farm, which is called the Bu (Old Norse *bú* meaning 'great hall') and was perhaps the centre of Kolbein Hruga's estate.

Above: St Mary's Chapel, possibly the final resting place of Cubbie Roo.

ST MAGNUS CHURCH

Egilsay

This is not the kirk where St Magnus prayed before his murder around 1116. It was built a few decades later, as a memorial to his martyrdom on the island.

The rectangular nave has doors to the south and north, and leads directly into the vaulted chancel with no chancel arch. Above the nave was a gallery which led into an attic above the chancel; this space may have been used to store valuables. There are windows to either side within the nave and chancel, though none are large. At the west end of the nave, a door leads to a tall round tower which was originally considerably higher than it is today, possibly up to five storeys high.

Towers such as this were a popular feature of many Norwegian churches, but this is the only example to survive in Orkney. Their purpose was defensive as well as stylistic. At St Magnus the tower can only be entered from the inside of the kirk and the windows are curiously arranged to the points of the compass: the ground floor window faces south; the first floor faces west; the second floor, east; on the third floor there are four windows, one to each direction. On Egilsay the tower would provide clear views of any approaching longships.

By the 19th century the upper storeys of the tower had become unsafe, and it was lowered to its present height. Early illustrations show the tower with a beehive-shaped roof of stone.

Above: St Magnus Church, Egilsay, with its distinctive round tower.

CROSS KIRK, TUQUOY

Westray

Cross Kirk was originally built as a modest chapel, related to a high-status Norse settlement nearby. It may be associated with one Hafliki Thorkelsson who may have lived in the area.

Above: A slab inscribed with Norse runes, found at the church.

Top right: Cross Kirk at Tuquoy, possibly built by Hafliki Thorkelsson, a supporter of Earl Rognvald.

The nave is separated from the vaulted chancel by a rounded chancel arch with gently inclined jambs. In the 17th century, Cross Kirk served as one of the parish churches of Westray and the nave was lengthened to accommodate a larger congregation.

Today the walls are ruinous, though in better repair in the original body of the kirk where the original doorway, a single arched window, and the chancel arch survive. The graveyard surrounds the kirk.

ST BONIFACE CHURCH

Papa Westray

In earlier times this was a bustling and important site, in contrast to the peaceful surroundings of today.

The church was built by the Norse in the 12th century, though there may perhaps have been an earlier Pictish foundation here, possibly the seat of the Pictish bishopric of Orkney. Two Pictish symbol stones with cross motifs have been discovered in the graveyard: one is now in the Orkney Museum in Kirkwall, the other in the National Museum of Scotland in Edinburgh. Traces of both Iron Age and Pictish settlement, including a large round house, have been excavated nearby.

The Norse kirk comprised a small rectangular chapel, and the wealth of the congregation is attested by a fine hogback gravestone which lies in the graveyard, to the east of the old chancel. Since then, however, the church has been much altered. The nave was extended to accommodate larger congregations in the 17th century and shortly after this the chancel was demolished to construct a family burial enclosure for the Traill family, local landowners.

Above: A family gathering at St Boniface Church in the 1920s.

RENAISSANCE

THE EARL'S PALACE, KIRKWALL

Mainland, central Kirkwall

Earl Patrick Stewart started work on his palace in 1601. He located it near the cathedral, and focused his plan around the existing complex of the recently rebuilt Bishop's Palace.

Earl Patrick had ambitious plans for his new home. He wished to reflect the most fashionable architecture of his time, and there are clear French influences in the design. It was to be an ornate building, with corner turrets, massive projecting oriel windows, high-pitched slate roofs, and a substantial triple-arched window that gave onto the great hall. For the construction Earl Patrick imported sandstone from Eday (to the annoyance of the landowner, who was not paid for this valuable resource).

The building is L-plan in shape and the interior was designed to reflect the same elegance as the exterior. A wide stairway led to the great hall on the first floor. Small chambers at the top of the stair were provided for household staff, on hand to serve their lord and his guests. The hall was a bright room, amply lit by the great south-facing window and the oriel bays on either side, and it was heated by two massive stone fireplaces in the north and west walls. This was the space within which most of the earl's public business would have been conducted.

At the far end a doorway led to private apartments including an outer chamber (referred to as a 'dining room' in an inventory of 1653), and a bedchamber. Elsewhere there were other chambers, including facilities for guests, and on the ground floor stood the kitchen with massive fireplace and ovens, alongside a range of cellars and storerooms.

Though the bare walls of the palace seem austere today, the 1653 inventory, compiled upon the occupation of the building by Cromwell's troops, provides some idea of the grandeur and luxury that visitors might have enjoyed in Earl Patrick's heyday. There is mention of feather beds, deep Arras hangings, silk coverings and quilts, a 'great' Turkey carpet, various types of table, and all the necessities of life such as candlesticks and chamber pots.

The entrance to the palace gave no doubt as to the aspirations of its builder; two fluted pillars flank the doorway, above which there were three carved panels with an inscription (now gone), the arms of Earl Patrick, and, above all, the royal coat of arms. Nevertheless, building work was carried out against a backdrop of difficult times for Orkney. Poor harvests threatened the survival of farmers, and increased taxation augmented their problems. Both Earl Patrick and his father Earl Robert are said to have used forced labour in the construction of their palaces and this was long remembered as a most unhappy period.

The Earl's Palace has been described as 'the most mature and accomplished piece of Renaissance architecture left in Scotland', but it did not serve Earl Patrick well. By 1606 he was heavily in debt and after the disastrous attempt by his son (another Robert) to restore the Stewart lands in Orkney, both were executed for treason in 1615. By this time the palace had been handed to the bishops of Orkney to be used as their main residence.

In 1643 the earldom of Orkney was granted to William, 7th Earl of Morton and he took over the lease of the complex. After a period of use by the Cromwellian garrison, by 1705 the buildings had fallen into disrepair, and were recorded as unfit for habitation. Within 40 years the roof had been stripped.

The building remained an imposing ruin at the heart of the town. In the 1870s the possibility of re-roofing and consolidating it to serve as a new sheriff's court was considered by the architect David Bryce. Despite the 19th-century fashion for gothic buildings, the work was never carried out.

Today the Earl's Palace sits alone, but originally Earl Patrick had intended to link it to the rest of the ancient complex at the heart of Kirkwall. He did carry out some work in the Bishop's Palace and there are indications that a brewhouse and other buildings may have linked the two. The complex was known as the Palace of the Yards.

Opposite: The flamboyant architecture of the Earl's Palace was designed to portray its owner, Earl Patrick, as a man of taste and sophistication.

THE EARL'S PALACE, BIRSAY

Mainland, 13 miles north of Stromness

The palace in Birsay was built by Earl Robert Stewart, half-brother of Mary Queen of Scots. Work started around 1569, a few years after he was made Sheriff of Orkney.

Earl Robert's first years in Orkney had been troublesome and he no doubt saw the construction of a fine palace as a statement of his power and status. His new residence introduced a degree of elegance to local architecture that had not been seen before.It contrasted greatly with buildings such as Noltland Castle, built only a few years previously and yet much more austere and defensive in nature.

The palace was designed around a courtyard. Large glazed and panelled windows looked down from the upper floor both to the outside and to the courtyard. There were three ranges of buildings, each of two storeys, with three-storey turrets in the corners. In deference to the continuing troubles of the times, the ground-floor windows were smaller and below them there were gun ports.

The complex was entered from the south, through a grandiose entrance above which an inscription announced the royal connections of Earl Robert.

Unfortunately, due to a mistake in his Latin syntax he proclaimed himself, rather than his father, to be king. This was later used as evidence of the family's treasonable intentions.

Initially the great hall occupied the south range, above the entrance, but it was moved to the north after completion of buildings there in the 1580s. Kitchens, cellars and storerooms were housed on the ground floor and personal accommodation above. The west range (looking out to sea and the sunset) contained a single long gallery, another innovation drawing on fashions further south.

An account by John Brand published in 1701 describes the fine panelling and painted ceilings and walls of the palace, and a plan drawn around the same time illustrates the facilities such as bowling greens and archery butts that were incorporated to the outside.

Earl Robert died in 1593, and before long his son, Earl Patrick, turned his attention to the creation of a new and more magnificent palace in Kirkwall. Despite its comforts, the palace at Birsay fell into disuse and by 1653 a report for the Earl of Morton recommended swift repair as it was falling into ruin.

Above: The Earl's Palace at Birsay was a grand and ostentatious undertaking, the first building of its kind in Orkney.

NOLTLAND CASTLE

Westray

This highly defensive stronghold was built around 1560 by Gilbert Balfour, a member of the new Scottish aristocracy. He was deeply involved in the political intrigue of his day and the castle's architecture reflects his troubled history.

Left: Noltland Castle, whose austerity of design stands in marked contrast to the palaces of the Stewart earls.

Noltland Castle is built to a Z-plan, with square towers to either side of the main block. The walls are over 2m thick and pierced by 71 gun ports. There are small windows for the upper floors.

The ground floor contained storerooms and a kitchen, as was conventional, but Balfour wished to incorporate some elegance and comfort into his creation and this is visible in the courtly apartments on the first floor. The great hall occupied the central block and family accommodation was housed in the four-storey tower to the north-east. An elegant curved stair with an elaborately carved newel post at its centre now leads to these rooms.

In 1571 Noltland Castle was seized for a short time by Earl Robert Stewart, and although Balfour regained it, he was not to settle here. He eventually fled to Sweden, where he continued meddling in politics, and in 1576 he was executed for treason. In 1592 the castle passed back to the Stewarts, becoming property of John Arnot (later Sheriff of Orkney), in 1606.

Unlike its grander counterparts in Mainland Orkney, Noltland Castle was long in use. In the 17th century a courtyard, containing less defensive buildings, was added to the south, and the footings of other, later, buildings may be seen outside this.

LADY KIRK, PIEROWALL

Westray

The foundations of the Lady Kirk in Pierowall were laid down in the 13th century, but most of the ruins date from extensive rebuilding around 1674. The church is surrounded by a graveyard which is still in use.

For much of its history, Pierowall was a thriving centre, and the rebuilding in the 17th century provided a fine church for the congregation. At this time the nave was enlarged and the chancel rebuilt as a 'laird's aisle'. Between the two is a wide chancel arch of sandstone. Curiously, the chancel is out of alignment with the nave.

Two fine 17th-century grave-slabs within the church attest to the wealth and aspirations of the local population. During the Norse period the sheltered harbour and favourable location made Pierowall an important centre. Remains from a large Norse cemetery with rich grave goods have been found in the dunes close to the village.

Left: The Lady Kirk, Pierowall, largely constructed in the 17th century on a 13th-century site.

SKAILL HOUSE

Mainland, 7 miles N of Stromness

This fine mansion is unusual in that it has been owned and occupied by the same family since it was first built in the 1620s. The first occupant was Bishop George Graham, who moved to Orkney from Dunblane in 1615. In 1850, his descendant William Graham Watt became the man credited with discovering Skara Brae.

The house has undergone considerable enlargement since Bishop Graham's day. The original two-storey house was mirrored by a second building to the south, creating a small courtyard between the two, and a further wing to the north contained offices and a tower. Additional work in the 19th and 20th centuries enlarged the central block, roofing over the original courtyard, and creating a new, and larger, courtyard to the north.

The result is a complex mansion. In addition to the house, there is also an 18th-century dovecot, a walled garden from the 19th century and a home farm steading.

There has been a long history of settlement in the area. It was the 7th Laird, William Graham Watt, who recognised that the ruins uncovered in the nearby dunes, during a great storm in 1850, might represent something unusual. He undertook excavation at the site to reveal the first houses of Skara Brae.

During renovation work in 1996, the remains of a medieval cemetery were uncovered and excavated to the south and east of the house. The cemetery was used from the 11th century to the 14th, suggesting the presence of a substantial Norse community. Place-name evidence also hints at Norse settlement: the word 'Skaill' indicates a Norse hall-house. To the north, excavations have uncovered considerable evidence of Norse activity, including a rich hoard of precious metals and a substantial dwelling near the bay. Prior to the construction of Skaill House there was a farm here, part of the estates of Earl Robert Stewart.

Over the years the house has seen many illustrious guests, including Lady Jane Franklin, wife of Sir John Franklin who led the ill-fated expedition in search of the North-West Passage in 1845. In 1780 it provided shelter for officers from HMS *Resolution*, becalmed in Orkney on the journey homeward after Captain James Cook's last voyage. In thanks for the help they were given they left behind a fine china dinner service, still displayed in the house.

Above: The imposing west façade of Skaill House, close to Skara Brae.

TANKERNESS HOUSE

Mainland, central Kirkwall

Standing in the heart of Kirkwall, Tankerness House was originally built as the archdeaconry for St Magnus Cathedral. It was later expanded as a merchant's residence and now houses the Orkney Museum.

The northern wing of Tankerness House was built by Gilbert Fulzie, Kirkwall's first Protestant priest. A former archdeacon, Fulzie converted the building into a family home, adding an armorial panel over the entrance bearing the date 1574.

In the 17th century, the house passed to a wealthy merchant family, the Baikies. In the 18th century they enlarged and remodelled the house, adding new wings. Further ranges to the south and east were added later. In 1968 Tankerness House was restored by Orkney Islands Council and today it houses the Orkney Museum, with displays on local history and prehistory, as well as recent culture.

At the rear of the house there is a large garden. In the past, this provided produce for the kitchen; today it is a peaceful haven from the bustle of Kirkwall.

In 2005 a small summerhouse was moved here from its original position near the harbour. The spire of this little folly is built from ballast taken from the brig *Revenge*, captained in the early 18th century by John Gow, a local man. After a brief and inglorious career as a pirate, Gow was captured and taken to London for execution.

His ship remained in Orkney, where the volcanic ballast was used to create the centrepiece for the provost's new garden. As the original location fell into disrepair, the summerhouse, known as the Groatie Hoose from the cowrie shells used to decorate it, was moved to this more public location.

RENDALL DOVECOTE

Mainland, 14 miles NW of Kirkwall

This beehive-shaped dovecote was built in the mid-17th century. Birds such as pigeons provided an important source of meat and eggs for wealthy families.

This dovecote was built to serve the needs of the family living in the nearby Hall of Rendall. The meat was regarded as a delicacy and the waste provided an important source of fertiliser for the fields. The building is circular with four projecting string courses made of slate, designed to stop rats from gaining access to the interior. The birds entered through the roof, and there are gaps in the walls inside, to provide nesting boxes.

Right: Rendall Dovecote, with its rat-resistant slate ridges.

RECENT TIMES

SCAPA FLOW VISITOR CENTRE

Lyness, Hoy

In 1919 Lyness became the Base HQ for Scapa Flow, replacing short-lived HQs at Scapa Pier near Kirkwall, and later at Longhope in Hoy. It went on to play an important role in the Second World War, as the base for the Home Fleet. As a result, there are many war remains visible today.

In times of war, the strategic position and sheltered conditions of Scapa Flow made it an excellent deep water anchorage, suitable both for maintenance and re-fuelling, as well as for housing the fleet between periods of action.

The pumping station at Lyness was first built in 1917. Coal-fired boilers powered steam pumps which pumped fuel from tankers into storage tanks. The former pump house now houses the Scapa Flow Visitor Centre, with displays on the wartime role of Scapa Flow, the internment and scuttling of the German fleet, and famous vessels such as HMS *Royal Oak*, HMS *Hampshire* and HMS *Vanguard*. Artefacts are displayed alongside books of reminiscences and other documents.

Originally there were four oil storage tanks. In 1936 the pumps were converted to oil, and 12 further tanks built. More tanks were dug into the hillside above in the 1940s. Today only one tank remains, one of the original ones, built in 1917. This is open to the public, and is worth visiting because of its size and interior metal structure. It houses a display of vehicles associated with Lyness during the war, together with a small video area. The interior of the tank has an extraordinary acoustic.

Nearby is the Lyness Naval Cemetery, where many of those who served from Scapa Flow are laid to rest. They include shore personnel, crew from HMS *Royal Oak*, HMS *Hampshire*, and HMS *Vanguard*, those who died at the Battle of Jutland, and Germans who died during the scuttling of the German fleet, as well as German aircrew from the Second World War.

Above: Field Marshall Bernard Montgomery is welcomed aboard the HMS *Tyne* by Captain Hutton at Scapa Flow in the run up to D-Day in June 1944.

Between the wars, Lyness was the base for the firms engaged in the salvage of the German fleet. Some of the massive sheds associated with this work, built of red corrugated sheeting, may still be seen today. During the Second World War they housed recreational facilities such as the NAAFI and a cinema.

Other buildings at Lyness included workshops for repairs and work on the boom defences, great metal nets which were used to keep submarines and other enemy craft out of the Flow. There were also depots, accommodation blocks and mess huts, decontamination stations, a telephone exchange and a control centre, squash courts and six football pitches. Many of the buildings survive, either as empty shells or converted for modern use.

It is difficult to imagine now, but in the past there were more than 12,000 personnel stationed here. A leaflet providing a self-guided trail around the remains is available from the visitor centre.

The harbour front at Lyness includes a rectangular paved extension known as the Golden Wharf. This was created in the Second World War to provide deep-water accommodation for naval vessels. Land was reclaimed using spoil excavated from the oil tanks on the hillside above. Apparently it acquired its name from the cost of construction work. The Golden Wharf now provides a berth for the inter-island ferry service. The longer quayside is in demand for the appliances associated with the burgeoning marine renewables industry.

The hill above Lyness, known as the Wee Fea, commands a great view of the anchorage. It housed the final, underground, storage tanks, and a variety of wartime emplacements. At the top of the road a large concrete building with small porthole-like windows is built into the side of the hill. It has a flat roof, on which sits a small brick extension with viewing slits. This was the Base HQ and Communications Centre for the naval base and it was named HMS *Proserpine*. From here the movements of all ships into and out of the Flow could be monitored. Entry is unsafe, but it is well worth visiting the location, both for the fantastic views and to examine the building from outside. At one point over 230 people worked up here.

The wartime personnel in Hoy required accommodation, facilities and recreation. Many were not used to living in such northern climes. Theatre and cinema became an important feature of life, both to combat ennui and to allow personnel to feel in touch with life elsewhere. On the road towards Longhope stand the remains of the old Garrison Theatre, built around 1942. The massive Nissen huts forming its body have long gone, but the handsome art deco frontage survives, now converted into a private house.

Lyness today is thriving thanks to developments in the generation of power from the waves. The waters around Orkney are well suited to the development of commercially viable marine renewable devices and the Golden Wharf provides plenty of space for the manufacture, maintenance and development of machinery. Current work seeks to regenerate the facilities of the naval base while preserving its most important features.

Above: A diving helmet used during salvage operations between the wars at Scapa Flow. It is now on display at the visitor centre.

DOUNBY CLICK MILL

Mainland, 12 miles NE of Stromness

This small mill was built around 1825. It represents a type of mill once common on individual farms around the Northern Isles.

The mill is built of dry-stone and roofed with flagstones overlain by turf. A single door, away from the burn, is opposed by a small opening on the opposite wall, to create a through draft to remove any remaining chaff. A stone-lined lade led the water under the building where a small horizontal water-wheel (or tirl) turned to power the mill stones located in the mill directly above. The tirl here is unusual in that it comprises two sets of paddles, one above the other.

When the mill was running, a wooden stick was set to knock against the hopper and release new grain, giving out the characteristic 'click' sound from which the name is derived. The stones are cased in wood and a chute leads to the meal box.

In the 1920s quarrying work for the nearby road cut off the original water supply so that the mill is now fed by piped water, allowing the mechanism to turn for short periods. Records show that when in operation the mill ground about a bushel (around 250kg) of grain per hour.

Above: The internal workings of Dounby Click Mill.

TORMISTON MILL

Mainland, 5 miles NE of Stromness

Tormiston Mill was built towards the end of the 19th century and is a good example of the larger vertical mills which were built to replace click mills. Larger mills could serve a whole estate and were better suited to the gentler topography and gradual watercourses of Orkney.

The mill building is three storeys high and includes a twin-vented kiln to dry the grain. The iron waterwheel has eight spokes and was overshot – set so that the water flows onto the top of the wheel. Water is led to the wheel in a fine stone aqueduct. The dam, built to control a head of water, can still be seen further upstream.

Inside the mill it is possible to view the machinery, though the building has been converted into a visitor centre for Maeshowe. There is a small display and a shop.

Left: Tormiston Mill, with its overshot waterwheel at the right.

BARONY MILL

Mainland, 13 miles N of Stromness

There are three mills at Boardhouse, of which only the most recent is still in operation. It is the only working watermill in Orkney, and produces ground barley, or beremeal.

Barony Mill was built in 1873 and is also known as Boardhouse Mill. It comprises a three-storey stone building with an overshot iron wheel. The building also houses a grain kiln. Grain is dried on the top floor before being husked and then ground through three pairs of stones on the first floor. When the mill is running to capacity the wheel requires 110,000 gallons of water per hour for power.

The existence of a mill belonging to the bishopric at Boardhouse is mentioned in the 16th century. In the early 19th century the *New Statistical Account* records four mills in the parish. The other mill buildings here formed part of a complex steading. One was a threshing mill, the other used for corn. The mill pond and sluice survive, together with the arrangements for channelling water. Other buildings include accommodation for the millers, stables, and cart sheds. The mill is open to the public, and meal may be bought here.

Left: The miller, W. Phillips, checking the grain in the drying kiln at Barony Mill, 1968.

CORRIGALL FARM MUSEUM

Mainland, 11 miles NE of Stromness

Sometime between 1730 and 1740, James Corrigall returned to his family farm, which had been rented out. The oldest building now standing dates from this time, but over the years this working farmstead has seen much alteration and addition.

James Corrigall built the dwelling house with its stone and turf roof. Originally, one end served as a byre for the animals, but in time this was converted into accommodation for the family alone and a new byre was built downhill.

The original 'but' – the living end of the dwelling house – has been divided into an 'oot-bye' behind the fire (a cool room where food and drink were stored and processed), and an 'in-bye' or kitchen/living room. In addition there is a parlour and a bedroom.

The new byre and barn at Corrigall has a small round grain kiln at one end. This was fuelled by peat cut from the family's peat bank on the hill above. Warm air from the fire was used to dry the newly harvested grain; kilns such as this were a common feature of Orkney farms, necessary given the uncertainties of the damp climate. Later in the 19th century a separate byre was built to stable the large working horses that were used on local farms. Uphill, above the steading, there is a small threshing mill, to which water was carried over the burn by an aqueduct.

Today Corrigall Farm houses a museum of farming life in the 19th century.

Top left: The well-preserved 18th-century byre at Corrigall.

KIRBUSTER MUSEUM

Mainland, 12 miles N of Stromness

Kirbuster is the only surviving example in northern Europe of a type of house that was once common: the firehouse, a dwelling where the hearth lies in the centre of the main room.

The house was built, or possibly refurbished from a pre-existing dwelling, in 1723. It is a building of some pretensions, being both spacious and well lit with windows. In addition, even at this early date, the animals were housed separately.

The house has since been extended to include a parlour and two bedrooms with box beds. In the centre of the original dwelling room, a low stone wall serves as a back to the hearth, which is vented through a wooden smoke hole in the roof. A recess in the wall houses a neuk bed, smaller recesses are shelved for storage, and an extension houses a cool room.

The steading is preserved as a museum and it provides a good idea of the lifestyle of more prosperous farming people. In front of the house a whalebone arch leads to a fine garden, and a small area of woodland lies behind, in which willow and elder were grown for tasks such as basket-making and home remedies. To either side there are outbuildings including a pigsty, a smithy, a barn with a corn drying kiln, and a larger barn with a display of implements.

Right: The free-standing central hearth at Kirbuster.

DENNIS HEAD LIGHTHOUSE & BEACON

North Ronaldsay

The Stevenson family, famous for their ingenuity in helping improve safety at sea, had a hand in both the 18th-century beacon and the 19th-century lighthouse at Dennis Head.

The beacon was built in 1789 as one of the first four lighthouses commissioned in Scotland. It is 21m high and cost £199 12s 6d. It was erected by local masons under the guidance of lighthouse engineer Thomas Smith from Edinburgh. He was assisted by his stepson, Robert Stevenson, who later founded a dynasty of lighthouse engineers.

Originally the beacon was topped by a state-of-the-art lantern with oil lamps and copper reflectors. In 1809 this was replaced by a stone ball because a new lighthouse had been built at Start Point in Sanday. Nevertheless, by 1852 there were plans to build a new lighthouse at Dennis Head and this was completed in 1854, again built by the Stevenson family.

This is the tallest land-based lighthouse in Britain. It is over 42m high and the cost was £681 8s 7d – regarded as particularly expensive at the time. While the old beacon is built of stone, the new lighthouse was constructed mainly of brick, on a stone foundation and with stone corbels to support the external gallery.

The remains at Dennis Head also include accommodation for lighthouse staff and walling for gardens and sheep. Lighthouse tours are available.

Above: The beacon at Dennis Head, seen from the air.

SHEEP DYKE

North Ronaldsay

North Ronaldsay Sheep Dyke was built around the island's coast in 1832 to contain the sheep to the shore where they graze, happily, on seaweed. It is thought to be the largest drystone construction built as a single entity anywhere in the world.

The dyke is 19km long and roughly 2m high. It was originally built at a time of economic downturn, after the collapse of the kelp industry. Today maintenance is undertaken communally, by those whose farmlands adjoin the dyke, though it is an increasingly difficult task given the vulnerability of the structure to winter storms.

North Ronaldsay sheep are a primitive breed, today classed as rare. Husbandry of the sheep is also a communal undertaking. The ewes are brought inside the dyke to feed on grass before lambing, and during shearing time the community work together to herd the animals into stone 'punds'.

Left: The sheep dyke in use in the 1920s.

HACKNESS BATTERY & MARTELLO TOWER

South Walls, Hoy

The battery and Martello tower at Hackness were built at a time when Britain was at war with both France and America. Although their guns never fired on an enemy, the strategic importance of Orkney made such defences essential.

The battery was built in 1813, with eight gun emplacements, a small barracks and an underground magazine. It was intended to guard the entrance to the sheltered anchorage of Longhope Bay from American privateers or Napoleonic invaders. Local masons quarried and prepared the stone, and construction was carried out by the Royal Engineers.

Above: The 64-pounder gun on the roof of the Martello tower.

Right: Sleeping quarters at the nearby battery, with ingenious foldaway beds.

The Martello tower was one of a pair added in 1814 on opposite sides of Longhope Sound. They were built to a robust and sophisticated design. The walls of the tower vary in thickness, economising on stone while maintaining the strength of the vulnerable seaward side. There was a first-floor entrance, via a retractable ladder, and once inside the garrison could survive for several days. The ground floor contained a water tank, storage, and the powder room, which was carefully ventilated and designed to minimise damage in the event of a blast. Accommodation was on the first floor. The top floor housed the gun emplacement, together with a system to collect water.

In 1866 the defences were remodelled and remanned in response to a potential Fenian invasion. The battery was enlarged with further accommodation and a bigger magazine. The guns were changed from eight 24-pounders to four 68-pound Armstrong cannon. The garrison comprised 20 officers and 50 men.

The Armstrong cannon was the most advanced gun of the time, but by the 1890s it was obsolete, and the guns were removed in the early 20th century. During the First World War, the Martello tower was used as a signal and semaphore station. Shortly after the war the battery was sold and converted into a farm steading.

During the Second World War Crockness Martello Tower, on the other side of Longhope Bay, was requisitioned as a weather station, while Hackness remained empty. Graffiti on the internal walls show that the towers were popular places to visit, both for the troops stationed in Hoy and for locals.

NESS BATTERY

Mainland, 0.5 mile SW of Stromness

Ness Battery is the only wartime battery in the UK where ranges of wooden accommodation huts survive. The mess hall features a unique mural depicting rural England. This is the best-preserved of the 20 coastal batteries that were built to defend Orkney during the Second World War.

The battery occupies an important position, guarding the western entrance into Scapa Flow. The first gun emplacements were built here in the First World War, though only their footings survive, within the golf course, about 200m south-east of the Second World War battery.

Work on Ness Battery started in 1938, in response to the Munich Crisis, when Hitler laid claim to parts of what is now the Czech Republic. It was reinforced in 1941. Two emplacements, each housing a massive 6in gun within a concrete shelter, look out over the Hoy Sound. Flat concrete roofs are suspended on a framework of steel beams to provide protection from air attack and blast for the gunners.

A two-storey observation tower stands slightly uphill, providing a good view of Scapa Flow. All shipping passing in and out of the Flow was checked by naval personnel and orders to fire could be issued when necessary. Behind the defences are underground magazines and shelters, though access to these is currently sealed off.

There are also wooden accommodation blocks, which had to be self-contained despite their proximity to Stromness. The mess hall features a remarkable mural depicting rural England, perhaps a reflection of the troops' origin. It shows a fertile green landscape rich with trees and flowers, in stark contrast with the landscape to which they had been posted. The mural is highly accomplished and is signed 'A.R. Woods', though the artist's identity has never been confirmed. The mess hall incorporated a theatre: some of the shows were open to local residents as well as the garrison.

After the war, some of the battery was cleared but the blocks at its heart were retained for use as a training camp by the Territorial Army. Since the mid-1990s it has fallen into disrepair, but recent restoration work has opened the site for public access.

Above: Part of the mural at Ness Battery, whose artist has never been traced.

Right: Royal Marine Artillery officers at Ness Battery around 1917.

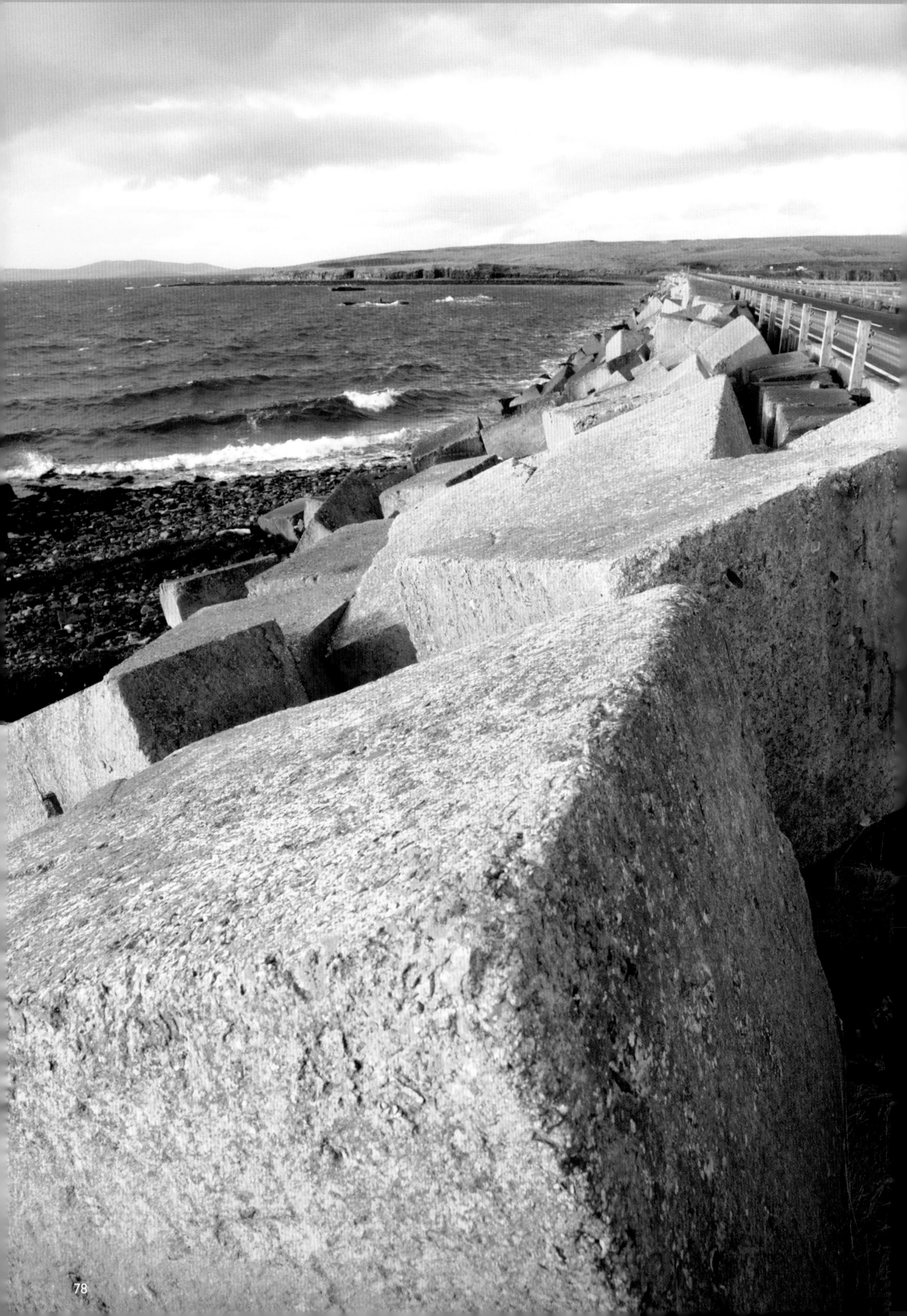

THE CHURCHILL BARRIERS

From Mainland, 7 miles SE of Kirkwall

At the beginning of the Second World War, a lethal U-boat attack exposed the vulnerability of Scapa Flow. Winston Churchill, then First Lord of the Admiralty, responded by commissioning unique and highly effective ranges of concrete and rubble defences, which now survive as causeways between the South Isles.

The defence of Scapa Flow was recognised as a problem in the First World War. Blockships, comprising old merchant vessels, were sunk in the eastern access channels to restrict marine traffic. The inadequacy of this measure was proved on 14 October 1939, when the German submarine U-47 slipped through Kirk Sound to torpedo HMS *Royal Oak* as she lay at anchor at the mouth to Scapa Flow.

Work began in May 1940 to build a series of solid barriers across the channels. Only two entrances, to the south and west, would be left open. The channels between the eastern islands were deep, with fast-running currents and tides of up to 12 knots, so the construction of the barriers was highly specialised.

The work was undertaken by Balfour Beatty using local, British and Irish workers, and, from 1942, prisoners of war. Metal gantries were constructed and aerial cableways (known as Blondins) were used to drop graded rubble and rock into the channels. Initially a scale model was made using a cattle trough as an experimental tank. The original plan was to use a rubble core, but the unconsolidated stone just washed away, so wire bolsters filled with rock were necessary. The final design of each barrier is a sophisticated layering of rubble between bolsters encased in concrete blocks. Blocks of different sizes were laid in different ways to dissipate the force of the tides.

The machinery used was on a scale not previously seen in Orkney. Four of the Blondins were brought to the UK from Iraq, where they had been used to construct a barrage across the River Tigris. They needed extending and strengthening for the work in Orkney. Small steam and diesel engines arrived and miles of track were laid, to transport material to the cableways. Quarries were opened to obtain rock, and five yards were built to cast the concrete blocks. Steam cranes were used at the blockyards and pierheads.

All of this needed servicing: coal, water, oil and sand were needed for the railways; food and accommodation for the workmen; transport by road and water was vital. It is surprising how little remains of this extraordinary infrastructure, but the machinery soon went back south. Only a few stretches of track and rusting wagons survive.

In total, over 66,000 concrete blocks were cast, using 333,000 tons of concrete. Over 580,000 tons of rock were quarried. The first channel to be closed was East Weddel, in May 1942. The last was Skerry Sound, in June 1943.

The use of prisoners of war as labour was controversial. After consultation at the highest level it was confirmed that projects that would benefit the community after the war were not to be defined as war work. For those who live in Orkney today, the benefits of the barriers are incalculable.

Left: Part of the mighty defences, commissioned by Winston Churchill to deny enemy ships access to Scapa Flow.

Right: Constructing bolsters for use in building the barriers, August 1941.

THE ITALIAN CHAPEL

Lamb Holm

Conjured up from unpromising materials by Italian prisoners of war working on the Churchill Barriers, this chapel is a remarkable and poignant survival from a bleak episode of the Second World War.

In 1942 a group of Italian prisoners arrived in Orkney to work on the construction of the Churchill Barriers. They had been captured in North Africa, and were housed in prison camps in Burray and Lamb Holm.

Despite the strenuous labour of building the barriers, the Italians worked to soften the stark surroundings of their camps. On Lamb Holm they planted flower beds and created facilities such as a theatre and a recreation hut. In 1943 they began work on a chapel for their camp.

The main structure comprised two Nissen huts, placed end to end. The prisoners used whatever raw materials they could lay their hands on. Some materials, such as timber, were salvaged from the wrecked blockships lying in the channels where they were working. Others were donated – such as plasterboard and spare paint – and some were scrounged, such as empty beef cans. The work was guided by Domenico Chiocchetti, a painter, but many prisoners had talents that were put to good use.

The ornate façade, with its belfry and porch supported on twin columns, contrasts with the starkness of the Nissen huts and hints at the grandeur inside. The interior is painted with remarkable realism to resemble carved stonework, with a dado and ornate columns. A wrought-iron rood screen encloses the sanctuary, with its concrete altar-rail and altar. Where the gates of the rood screen join, a wrought-iron heart in the floor is reputed to commemorate the love affair between a prisoner and a local girl. Behind the altar, Chiocchetti painted a Madonna and Child, replicating a painting by Nicolo Barabino, a copy of which he had kept with him.

Chiocchetti remained for a short period after the war, to complete work on the chapel, but the disused camp was soon to be cleared. Fortunately the chapel was spared, and in the 1960s many of the original artists were traced, including Chiocchetti. Repair work was organised, carried out by returning Italians and local people, and the chapel was restored to its original glory.

Chiocchetti came from Moena, a small town in northern Italy, and the connections continue. Children from local schools, musical and other groups all make exchange trips.

The chapel is dedicated to the Queen of Peace. It stands above the footings of the camp and is much visited, both as a tourist destination and for services, weddings and concerts. Outside stands another of Chiocchetti's creations, a statue of St George, which he created from cement laid over a barbed-wire frame. It is a powerful evocation of our ability to create our own heritage.

Top: The Italian prisoners of war outside the chapel, with Domenico Chiocchetti standing far left.

Left: Chiochetti's statue of St George.

NATURAL
HISTORY

THE NATURAL HISTORY OF ORKNEY

Orkney's natural history is underpinned by its geological past. Four hundred million years ago, there was a vast lake covering an area from the Moray Firth to Norway. During this time sediment, mud and sand were deposited, and later became the sandstone, siltstone and mudstone which underlies most of Orkney.

These 'flagstone' rock formations have been eroded along the west coast by the rolling Atlantic waves, creating the spectacular cliffs, sea-stacks, caves and geos. Fossils are found at many sites on Orkney: the Bay of Skaill by Skara Brae is particularly important. Plant fossils found here play a vital role in the understanding of plant evolution during a period when land plants were only just appearing. However, visitors should be aware that the fossils are protected by law and should not be removed.

COASTAL WILDLIFE

The sea cliffs of Orkney provide spectacular scenery, but the ledges also make perfect nesting sites for thousands of seabirds. In the early summer, the cliffs are a raucous spectacle, when fulmars, kittiwakes, razorbills and guillemots compete for nesting sites on precarious ledges.

Marwick Head, near the Brough of Birsay, is a towering example of Orkney's sheer cliffs. As well as the more numerous species, look out for Arctic skua and great skua (or bonxie), both of which mob other gulls to make them throw up their food, and rare species such as the glaucous gull and Icelandic gull. When visiting Westray or Birsay look out for puffin too.

The Royal Society for the Protection of Birds owns or manages large areas of Orkney, including the land surrounding the Ring of Brodgar. Here you can see oystercatchers, lapwing and curlews – known by Orcadians as whaups – with their distinctive curved beaks. More often heard than seen is the skylark, or teeick – its beautiful song heard from on high.

Opposite: An otter. These nocturnal mammals are seen at shorelines all over Orkney.

Right: A puffin, with its distinctive, brightly coloured bill. Puffins are often seen around Westray and Birsay.

Wild mammals are common around Orkney's coastlines. Seals both grey and common can be seen regularly. These curious animals are often seen in the Loch of Stenness and at Eynhallow Sound near the Broch of Gurness. Dolphins, porpoises and whales are also sometimes sighted near Gurness. Seventeen species of marine mammal have been reported swimming in the waters around Orkney – including minke, sperm, humpback, killer and beluga whales.

Patient observers at Stenness Loch and Harray Loch may be rewarded with a sighting of an otter. Otters are nocturnal, so keen observers should try dawn or dusk if they want to see them. Otters eat fish and crabs so they are seen both in fresh water and salt water. They can sometimes be spotted hunting along the rocky, seaweed-strewn shores.

The windswept shores of Orkney provide a tough environment for plants. The Scottish primrose is only found in Orkney, Caithness and Sutherland. This small, seemingly delicate flower flourishes here because it can tolerate nutrient-poor soils and the buffeting of strong, salt-laden winds. A good place to find it is along the Yesnaby cliffs. At the Brough of Birsay other coastal flowers are common. Pink thrift grows in clumps along the shoreline and the delicate blue/violet spring squill grows in the coastal grassland.

NATURAL HISTORY: INLAND WILDLIFE

Although much of Orkney is a coastal landscape, there are important habitats further inland, providing unique conditions where certain species thrive.

Among the most remarkable creatures found here is the Orkney vole. This species is similar to the common vole, but larger and darker. Although it probably originated in continental Europe, the Orkney vole is not found elsewhere in the British Isles. It is thought to have arrived from what is now France or Spain around 2600 BC, during Orkney's Neolithic heyday. Its size varies slightly between different island populations: the voles of Westray are supposed to be the smallest and darkest. Voles can be difficult to see, but their runs are quite easily spotted amid the long grass and heather covering the chambered tombs of Cuween and Wideford.

Brown hares were first introduced to Orkney by the Liberal MP and science writer Samuel Laing (1812–97). Over the years they were introduced to Hoy, Eday, Rousay, Shapinsay, South Ronaldsay, Westray and Papa Westray. Today they are mainly found on the Mainland. In 1955 *The Orcadian* newspaper recorded the export of 3 tonnes of hares (about 800 animals) to Germany.

The mountain hare is found only on Hoy. This species turns white in winter and in summer it can be distinguished from the brown hare by its white tail.

Orkney is a good place to see the rare great yellow bumblebee and the moss carder bee. Although they are found all over Orkney, one of their favourite habitats is around the Ring of Brodgar. The moss carder bee was once widespread, but is now restricted to tall, open grasslands close to the sea. Queens emerge from March to May and start to search for nest sites. The nest is built on or just under the ground, covered by moss or dry grass collected by the bees; hence the name 'carder' bee.

The Ring of Brodgar sits within a specially managed wildflower meadow, which is vibrant with colour throughout the spring and summer. Among the flower species to be seen are yellow rattle, heath violet, purple lousewort, northern marsh orchid and the delicate pale pink heath spotted orchid. Bird's-foot trefoil also grows here, and is a particular favourite of bumblebees.

Above: A moss carder bee, often seen around the Ring of Brodgar.

Above: An Orkney vole, a subspecies of the European common vole, not found in any other part of the British Isles.

This page: Mountain hare, found only on the island of Hoy, shown here with its distinctive white winter coat.

Historic Scotland Membership offers fantastic days out all year, plus many other benefits, discounts and special offers. Membership is available for 12 months or for life, in a variety of different categories.

MEMBERSHIP BENEFITS

- Entry to over 300 Historic Scotland sites as often as you want
- Quarterly membership magazine
- Member discount in Historic Scotland's shops, both online and at individual sites
- Access to over 500 historic sites in the care of English Heritage, Cadw (Wales) and Manx National Heritage (Isle of Man) paying half-price entry for the first year, then free thereafter

HOW TO JOIN

There are four ways you can obtain more information or start your membership:

In person: At any staffed Historic Scotland site or property.

By phone: Call +44(0)131 668 8999 with your credit/debit card details.

Online: www.historic-scotland.gov.uk/member

By post to: Historic Scotland Membership, Longmore House, Salisbury Place, Edinburgh EH9 1SH.

EXPLORER PASS

For visitors to Scotland, the Explorer Pass offers admission to all Historic Scotland properties for 3 or 7 days. Ask for details and prices at any Historic Scotland property or visit our website at www.historic-scotland.gov.uk/explorer

FURTHER READING AND CREDITS

L. Burgher, *Orkney: an Illustrated Architectural Guide* (1991)

S. Foster, *Maeshowe and the Heart of Neolithic Orkney* (2006)

T. Muir, *The Shorter Orkneyinga Saga* (2006)

T. Muir (ed), *Orkney in the Sagas* (2006)

H. Palsson & P. Edwards (translators) *The Orkneyinga Saga* (2004)

P. Paris, *Orkney's Italian Chapel, the true story of an icon* (2010)

G. Stell, *Orkney at War: Defending Scapa Flow, Part 1 World War One* (2011)

W.P.L. Thomson, *A New History of Orkney* (2008)

C.R. Wickham-Jones, *Between the Wind and the Water: World Heritage Orkney* (2006)

C.R. Wickham-Jones, *Orkney: a Historical Guide* (2011)

Historic Scotland also provides detailed guidebooks to several of its sites in Orkney.

The Orkney poet George Mackay Brown wrote numerous stories set among the antiquities of Orkney and all are a good read. A complete list of his works may be found on www.georgemackaybrown.co.uk

Websites
www.orkneyjar.com
www.orkneycommunities.co.uk

First published by Historic Scotland 2012
Printed from sustainable materials 2012
Crown copyright © Historic Scotland 2012
ISBN 978-1-84917-073-4

Editor: Andrew Burnet
Design: Contagious UK Ltd
Natural history text, pp. 83–4: Bob Tevendale
Principal photography: Historic Scotland Photo Unit
Illustrations p.6, p.9, p.10, p.11, p.20 and p.36: Brian Lee
Passages from *Orkneyinga Saga: The History of the Earls of Orkney* translated by Hermann Pálsson and Paul Edwards. Published by The Hogarth Press and reprinted by permission of The Random House Group Limited.

FINDING THE MONUMENTS

Sites are listed by island, then alphabetically. The numbers given refer to the map on page 89.

An admission charge is payable at sites marked (£). Note that some sites close for the winter.

For general information, particularly about ferry crossings and access to remote sites, contact VisitOrkney, 01856 872 856.

Sites marked (HS) are run by Historic Scotland. For general information contact Skara Brae, 01856 841 815.

MAINLAND

1 Barnhouse Village
Near the Stones of Stenness, off the B9055.
OS: HY 308 127
Page 32

2 Barony Mill (also known as Boardhouse Mill)
At Birsay, off the A967.
OS: HY 255 275
Tel: 01856 721 439
Page 73

3 Bishop's Palace (HS)
In central Kirkwall. (£)
OS: HY 449 108
Tel: 01856 871 918
Page 56

4 Broch of Gurness (HS)
Near Evie off the A966. (£)
OS: HY 382 269
Tel: 01856 751 414
Page 38

5 Brough of Birsay (HS)
Via a tidal causeway at Birsay, off the A967. (£)
OS: HY 240 285
Tel: 01856 841 815
(Skara Brae) for tide times.
Page 58

6 Brough of Deerness
At the eastern tip of Mainland, off the B9050.
OS: HY 596 087
Page 59

7 Churchill Barriers
Forming the A961, running south from St Mary's.
OS: HY 474 014
Page 78

8 Corrigall Farm Museum
In Harray off the A986.
OS: HY 324 193
Tel: 01856 771 411
Page 74

9 Cuween Hill Chambered Cairn (HS)
Near Finstown, on a minor road off the A965.
OS: HY 364 128
Page 49

10 Dounby Click Mill (HS)
East of Dounby off the B9057.
OS: HY 325 228
Page 72

11 Earl's Bu (HS)
At Orphir off the A964.
OS: HY 335 044
Page 60

12 Earl's Palace, Birsay (HS)
At Birsay on the A966.
OS: HY 248 278
Page 66

13 Earl's Palace, Kirkwall (HS)
In central Kirkwall. (£)
Tel: 01856 871 918
OS: HY 450 108
Page 64

14 Grain Earth House (HS)
West of Kirkwall in the Hatston Industrial Estate off the A965.
OS: HY 442 116
Page 37

15 Kirbuster Museum
Near Twatt off the A986/A967.
OS: HY 283 254
Tel: 01856 771 268
Page 74

16 Knowes of Trotty
Near Harray, south of moorland road off the A986.
OS: HY 342 174
(Car park: HY 334 164)
Page 53

17 Maeshowe (HS)
Near Stenness on the A965. (£)
OS: HY 318 128
Tel: 01856 761 606
Page 46

18 Mine Howe
At Toab, Tankerness, south-east of Kirkwall off the A960. (£)
OS: HY 511 060
Tel: 01856 861 234
Page 45

19 Ness Battery
South of Stromness off the A965. Accessible only by guided tour. (£)
OS: HY 249 080
For details contact Visit Orkney on 01856 872 856.
Page 77

20 Ness of Brodgar
North of Stennes on the B9055.
Tours are likely to be available while summer excavations continue, in July and August.
OS: HY 303 129
Page 44

21 Orphir Round Kirk (HS)
At Orphir on the A964.
OS: HY 335 044
Page 60

22 Rendall Dovecote
Near Tingwall on the east coast, off the A966.
OS: HY 423 207
Page 69

23 Rennibister Earth House (HS)
In a farmyard off the A965.
OS: HY 397 126
Page 37

24 Ring of Brodgar (HS)
North of Stenness on the B9055.
OS: HY 295 134
Page 42

25 Skaill House
In Skaill Bay on the west coast, off the B9056. (Joint ticket with Skara Brae.)
OS: HY 234 186
Tel: 01856 841 501
Page 68

26 Skara Brae (HS)
In Skaill Bay on the west coast, off the B9056. (£)
OS: HY 231 187
Tel: 01856 841 815
Page 30

27 St Magnus Cathedral
In central Kirkwall.
OS: HY 449 109
Tel: 01856 874 894
Page 54

28 Stones of Stenness (HS)
North of Stenness on the B9055.
OS: HY 307 125
Page 40

29 Tankerness House (Orkney Museum)
In central Kirkwall.
OS: HY 449 109
Tel: 01856 873 191
Page 69

30 Tormiston Mill (HS)
At Stenness on the A965.
OS: HY 319 126
Tel: 01856 761 606
Page 73

31 Unstan Chambered Cairn (HS)
On the south bank of the Loch of Stenness, off the A965/A964.
OS: HY 283 117
Page 48

32 Wideford Hill Chambered Cairn (HS)
From the Old Finstown Road, via Heathfield Farm and a long hillwalk.
OS: HY 409 121
Page 49

EDAY
(via air or ferry from Kirkwall)

**33 Vinquoy
Chambered Cairn**
At the north of the island.
OS: HY 560 381
Page 52

EGILSAY
(via ferry from Tingwall)

34 St Magnus Church (HS)
Near the centre of
the island.
OS: HY 466 304
Page 62

EYNHALLOW
(by private hire boat only)

35 Eynhallow Church (HS)
On the south coast of
the island, accessible
by private hire boat.
OS: HY 359 288
Tel: 01856 841 815
(Skara Brae)
Page 61

HOY
(via ferry from Houton)

36 Dwarfie Stane (HS)
At the north end of the
island, off the road from
Moaness to Rackwick.
OS: HY 243 004
Page 53

**37 Hackness Battery and
Martello Tower (HS)**
At the eastern tip of the
South Walls peninsula,
off the B9047. (£)
OS: ND 338 913
Tel: 01856 701 727
Page 76

**38 Scapa Flow
Visitor Centre**
At Lyness, on the B9047.
OS: ND 310 943
Tel: 01856 791 300
Page 70

LAMB HOLM
(via the Churchill
Barriers causeway)

39 Italian Chapel
At the north of the island,
off the A961.
OS: HY 488 006
Tel: 01856 781 268
Page 80

NORTH RONALDSAY
(via air or weekly ferry
from Kirkwall)

**40 Dennis Head
Lighthouse and Beacon**
At the north-eastern tip
of the island.
OS: HY 784 560
Page 75

41 Sheep Dyke
Around most of the island.
OS: HY 765 540
Page 75

PAPA WESTRAY
(via air or ferries from
Kirkwall and Westray)

**42 Holm of Papa
Westray (HS)**
A tiny islet to the east of
the island, accessible only
by private boat.
OS: HY 509 518
Page 52

43 Knap of Howar (HS)
On the west coast
of the island.
OS: HY 483 518
Page 33

44 St Boniface Church
In the middle of the
island off the main road.
OS: HY 488 527
Page 63

ROUSAY
(via ferry from Tingwall)

**45 Blackhammer Stalled
Cairn (HS)**
On the B9064 at the
south of the island.
OS: HY 414 276
Page 50

46 Knowe of Yarso (HS)
On the B9064 at the
south of the island.
OS: HY 405 280
Page 51

47 Midhowe Broch (HS)
At the south-west of
the island.
OS: HY 372 306
Page 39

**48 Midhowe Stalled
Cairn (HS)**
At the south-west of
the island.
OS: HY 372 305
Page 50

**49 Taversöe Tuick
Chambered Cairn (HS)**
On the B9064 at the
south of the island.
OS: HY 426 276
Page 51

SANDAY
(via air or ferry from Kirkwall)

50 Meur Burnt Mound
Near Sandquoy at the
north-east of the island.
OS: HY 747 457
Page 35

**51 Quoyness Chambered
Cairn (HS)**
On the Quoy Ness
peninsula to the south
of the island's centre.
OS: HY 677 378
Page 52

52 Tofts Ness
At the northern tip
of the island.
OS: HY 760 470
Page 36

SHAPINSAY
(via ferry from Kirkwall)

53 Burroughston Broch
Near the north-east tip of
the island, off the B9058.
OS: HY 541 210
Page 39

SOUTH RONALDSAY
(via the Churchill Barriers,
15 miles south of Kirkwall)

**54 Isbister
Chambered Cairn**
At Liddle Farm, signed 'Tomb
of the Eagles' off the B9041
at the south of the island. (£)
OS: ND 470 845
Tel: 01856 831 339
Page 48

55 Liddle Burnt Mound
See 54 above.
OS: ND 465 842
Page 35

WESTRAY
(via air or ferry from Kirkwall)

56 Cross Kirk, Tuquoy (HS)
At the Bay of Tuquoy,
off the B9067.
OS: HY 455 432
Page 63

**57 Lady Kirk,
Pierowall (HS)**
In Pierowall.
OS: HY 439 488
Page 67

58 Links of Noltland (HS)
Near Pierowall off
the B9066.
OS: HY 428 493
Page 34

59 Noltland Castle (HS)
Near Pierowall off
the B9066.
OS: HY 429 487
Page 67

60 Quoygrew
At the north of the island
near Rackwick.
OS: HY 443 507
Page 60

WYRE
(via ferry from Tingwall)

**61 Cubbie Roo's
Castle (HS)**
Near the centre of
the island.
OS: HY 442 263
Page 57

62 St Mary's Chapel
Near the centre of
the island.
OS: HY 443 263
Page 61